Isaac Asimov
A Checklist of Works Published in the
United States, March 1939--May 1972

Isaac Asimov

A Checklist of Works Published in the United States, March 1939--May 1972

By Marjorie M. Miller

With a Note by
Isaac Asimov

The Kent State University Press

The Serif Series: *Number 25*

Bibliographies and Checklists

William White, General Editor
Wayne State University

ISBN 0-87338-126-2
Library of Congress Card Catalog Number 72-76948
Manufactured in the United States of America
at the press of the Oberlin Printing Company
Design by Merald E. Wrolstad
First Edition

Looking over the manuscript of the bibliography of my works prepared by Mrs. Miller fills me with a sense of guilt and more than a small bit of fright. I had no intention, ever, of presenting the insuperable problem to bibliographers that I have apparently succeeded in doing. If, when I first began writing for publication, at the age of 18, some guardian angel had whispered in my ear: "By mid-1972, you must have written enough to fill 122 books and have a bibliography which, in English, must fill sixty-five typewritten pages," I would have run from my typewriter screaming and never approached it again. —But little by little and page by page it was all done, and, just between us, I am continuing to pile it up even right now. I have at least twelve books in press and scheduled for 1972 and 1973 publication. Others are in preparation and of course there are shorter pieces in the works, too. —I apologize, Mrs. Miller.

——Isaac Asimov

Contents

Introduction

Dr. Asimov's work presents some unusual problems for the bibliographer. First, there is the sheer volume of it; Doubleday, one of his major publishers, reports that he writes eight hours a day, seven days a week, and the quantity of material he publishes makes this easy to believe. The second problem stems from the diversity of both his writing and his markets. Most of his early work was science fiction, but since 1958 he has concentrated more and more of his efforts on science popularization, science books and articles for children, and works on literature and history. He publishes in a wide variety of periodicals, from *Amazing Stories* and the *Journal of Chemical Education* to *TV Guide*, *Boys' Life*, and *Mademoiselle*. Many of his early stories appeared in science fiction magazines that are found in very few libraries; some of his later works have appeared in specialized publications, such as *Lithopinion*, which are difficult to locate. Some of these periodicals are not included in any of the standard indexes. He has also contributed many articles, stories, essays, and introductions to books written and edited by others, and has written for several encyclopedias. Finding these can be almost as much a matter of luck as of diligent search.

The present checklist is limited to works published in the United States, with the exception of British and Canadian editions of Asimov's books. Where such editions have come to my attention, they have been included, but it has not been possible to make an exhaustive search for them. No translations or other foreign editions are included although many of his books have been translated; neither have any foreign periodicals been surveyed. The listings end with May 1972, except for the inclusion of some books published or scheduled for publication after that date.

Data on reprintings and revised and new editions of books, and anthology appearances of stories, are as complete as possible. Science fiction anthologies are notoriously ephemeral, and there are surely many that have been missed. Those that appear, however, provide a good picture of which stories have been the most popular and most durable in appeal.

Almost all of the entries have been verified either personally, or by helpful magazine editors, librarians, and science fiction fans. The few entries that remain unverified are incomplete— page numbers or volume numbers are missing. Entries for books list any periodical publication of the material, then subsequent editions and reprintings in chronological order, including reprintings under new titles. Periodical entries list any further periodical appearances first; then book publications, if any, and appearances in Asimov collections; appearances in other anthologies are then listed in chronological order. All fiction works are indicated by an F in the left margin.

The second part of this checklist is devoted to selected criticism and works about Asimov. There is no well-defined body of literary criticism dealing with the work of a man who, like Asimov, writes science fiction and popular non-fiction. To be considered a "major literary figure," worthy of study and criticism, one must write "serious" novels. With a few exceptions, criticism in the science fiction field proves to consist of defining science fiction, retelling its history, or debating its significance, either as literature or as prophecy and social criticism.

Brief comments about Asimov's work can be found throughout almost everything written about science fiction since the early forties. Most of it deals with the robot stories, the Three Laws of Robotics, and the *Foundation* series. These are generally regarded as his major contributions to the development of science fiction in the United States and are frequently cited as landmarks or watersheds in the history of the genre. Asimov's Three Laws have taken on an independent reality of their own because they have been used, either explicitly or implicitly, by so many other writers. For example, Murray Leinster, in "The Case of the Homicidal Robots," says "they could not directly harm nor indirectly injure nor stand aside inactive while a human being was being hurt."[1] Asimov's Galactic Empire concept is also used by other science fiction writers as a framework for their stories.

Book reviews have not been included here because a list of the reviews of Asimov's 122 titles would be extremely long. Since most of the reviews have been of the short, utilitarian type, such a list would not be very significant. Reviews of his science fiction and science popularization have been predominantly favorable. Critical reception of his historical and literary works, on the other hand, has ranged from good through lukewarm to unfavorable. J. H. Crouch, reviewing *Asimov's Guide to Shakespeare* for *Library Journal*, says "As a director of Shakespeare's plays I shall find these volumes invaluable . . . helpful and interesting. . . . The style generally is good,"[2] while Benjamin DeMott, in the *Saturday Review*, says that the books have "value of a negative kind" because the likelihood of their eager adoption by schools and colleges is a sure sign of the great need for a change in the way English is being taught.[3]

[1] Ed Ferman, ed., *Once and Future Tales* (New York, 1968), p. 270.
[2] XCV (October 1, 1970), 3263.
[3] LIII (November 7, 1970), 46.

xii

Asimov is generally considered to be at his best when he is explaining a scientific concept in terms the layman can understand. *Choice* calls him "a master explainer; accurate, profound, and at the same time exciting."[4] Martin Green was expressing a minority opinion when he wrote, "Isaac Asimov has done some good work in science-for-the-layman, but there are times when he makes me feel I am curled up in my cradle, and a twinkly man in a white coat is teaching me to count— 'one . . . two . . . that's right' by pinching my little fingers one after the other. He may stand as a symbol of all those who make this kind of mistake."[5]

The selected list of critical works contains those treating Asimov at any length and a representative sampling of other types of writing about him—biographical sketches, bibliographies, essays occasioned by the publication of *Opus 100*, fanzine articles on Asimov the jolly-good-fellow, and one unpublished thesis. There have been a number of theses, according to Dr. Asimov himself; the one included here was simply the easiest to locate and annotate.

The index lists all Asimov titles with dates of first publication, but does not include introductions, forewords, and letters to editors, nor encyclopedia articles.

No project of this type could be carried out successfully without help and cooperation from numerous people, and this one is no exception. I would like to express my appreciation to Dr. Myron Lounsbury and Dr. Jackson Bryer of the University of Maryland, who helped me through the early confusions and difficulties; Neil Goble; Dr. Robert Rozman; M. B. Tepper; Malcolm Willits; the Prince George's County Memorial Library and the Library of Congress, where most of the research was

---

4 VII (May 1970), 404.
5 "Science and Sensibility: 1. Science for the layman. 2. Science fiction," *Kenyon Review*, XXV (Autumn 1963), 703.

done; many magazine and encyclopedia editors; Jo Zuppan of The Kent State University Press; Dr. Asimov himself, who has been unfailingly helpful; and my husband and children, without whose cooperation and encouragement nothing could have been accomplished.

Marjorie M. Miller

Shortened Periodical Titles

Amazing	*Amazing Stories*
Astonishing	*Astonishing Stories*
Astounding	*Astounding Science Fiction*
Beyond	*Beyond Fantasy Fiction*
Fantastic	*Fantastic Story Magazine*
F&SF	*Magazine of Fantasy and Science Fiction*
Future	*Future Science Fiction*
Galaxy	*Galaxy Science Fiction*
If	*If: Worlds of Science Fiction*
Infinity	*Infinity Science Fiction*
J.C.E.	*Journal of Chemical Education*
Marvel	*Marvel Science Stories*
Original	*The Original Science Fiction Stories*
Satellite	*Satellite Science Fiction*
Sci Di	*Science Digest*
Universe	*Universe Science Fiction*
Venture	*Venture Science Fiction*

I. Chronological Listing of Works by Isaac Asimov

1939

F "Marooned Off Vesta," *Amazing*, XIII (March), 66–77.
    Amazing, XXXIII (March 1959), 8–23.
    Asimov's Mysteries, 1968, pp. 125–140.
    Joseph Ross, ed. *The Best of Amazing*. Garden City, N.Y.:
    Doubleday, 1967, pp. 89–106.

  "Meet the Authors," *Amazing*, XIII (March), 126.
    Amazing, XXXIII (March 1959), 7.

F "The Weapon Too Dreadful to Use," *Amazing*, XIII (May),
    110–122.
    Early Asimov, 1972

F "Trends," *Astounding*, XXIII (July), 33–46.
    Early Asimov, 1972
    Martin Greenberg, ed. *Men Against the Stars*. New York: Gnome,
    1950, pp. 13–34. T. E. Dikty, ed. *Great S F Stories About the
    Moon*. New York: Fell, 1967, pp. 177–200. Hal Clement, ed.
    First Flights to the Moon. Garden City, N.Y.: Doubleday, 1970,
    pp. 40–63.

1940

F "Half-Breed," *Astonishing*, I (February), 38–53.
    Early Asimov, 1972
    Sam Moskowitz, ed. *The Space Magicians*. New York: Pyramid,
    1971, pp. 100–122.

F "Ring Around the Sun," *Future*, I (March), 89–98.
Early Asimov, 1972

F "Callistan Menace," *Astonishing*, I (April), 66–77.
Early Asimov, 1972 Excerpt, *Opus 100*, 1969, pp. 5–6.

F "The Magnificent Possession," *Future*, I (July), 71–81.
Early Asimov, 1972

F "Homo Sol," *Astounding*, XXVI (September), 117–131.
Early Asimov, 1972
Groff Conklin, ed. *Omnibus of Science Fiction*. New York: Crown, 1952, pp. 214–229.

F "Strange Playfellow," *Super Science Stories*, I (September), 67–77.
I, Robot, 1950, pp. 17–40, under the title "Robbie." Excerpt, *Opus 100*, 1969, p. 61.
Judith Merril, ed. *Shot in the Dark*. New York: Bantam, 1950, pp. 183–197, under the title "Robbie." Groff Conklin, ed. *S.F. Thinking Machines*. New York: Vanguard, 1954, pp. 15–33.

F "Half-Breeds on Venus," *Astonishing*, II (December), 6–24.
Early Asimov, 1972

1941

F "The Secret Sense," *Cosmic Stories*, I (March), 87–95.
Early Asimov, 1972
Sam Moskowitz, ed. *Futures to Infinity*. New York: Pyramid, 1970, pp. 167–180.

F "History," *Super Science Stories*, II (March), 86–93.
Early Asimov, 1972

F "Heredity," *Astonishing*, II (April), 8–25.
Early Asimov, 1972
Frederik Pohl, ed. *Beyond the End of Time*. Garden City, N.Y.: Doubleday, 1952, pp. 45–76.

F "Reason," *Astounding*, XXVII (April), 33–45.
> *I, Robot*, 1950, pp. 63–84.
>
> Damon Knight, ed. *A Century of Science Fiction*. New York: Simon & Schuster, 1962, pp. 26–41.

F "Liar!" *Astounding*, XXVII (May), 43–55.
> *I, Robot*, 1950, pp. 111–132. Excerpt, *Opus 100*, 1969, p. 62. Judith Merril, ed. *Human?* New York: Lion, 1954, pp. 138–158. Sam Moskowitz, ed. *Modern Masterpieces of Science Fiction*. Cleveland: World, 1965, pp. 295–315. Laurence M. Janifer, ed. *Masters' Choice*. New York: Simon & Schuster, 1966, pp. 15–33. Sam Moskowitz, ed. *Doorway Into Time*. New York: McFadden-Bartell, 1966, pp. 117–133. R. Silverberg, ed. *Mind to Mind: Nine Stories of Science Fiction*. New York: Nelson, 1971

F "Superneutron," *Astonishing*, III (September), 36–43.
> *Early Asimov*, 1972 Excerpt, *Opus 100*, 1969, p. 147.

F "Nightfall," *Astounding*, XXVIII (September), 9–34.
> *Nightfall and Other Stories*, 1969, pp. 2–36.
>
> Robert J. Healy & J. Francis McComas, eds. *Adventures in Time and Space*. New York: Random House, 1946, pp. 378–411. John W. Campbell, ed. *Astounding S F Anthology*. New York: Simon & Schuster, 1952, pp. 105–136. Damon Knight, ed. *Beyond Tomorrow*. New York: Harper & Row, 1965, pp. 173–228. Robert Silverberg, ed. *The Mirror of Infinity: A Critics' Anthology of Science Fiction*. New York: Harper & Row, 1970, pp. 49–91. Robert Silverberg, ed. *Science Fiction Hall of Fame*. Garden City, N.Y.: Doubleday, 1970, pp. 112–143.

F "Not Final," *Astounding*, XXVIII (October), 49–61.
> *Early Asimov*, 1972
>
> Groff Conklin, ed. *Possible Worlds of S F*. New York: Vanguard, 1951, pp. 79–95. Arthur C. Clarke, ed. *Time Probe: The Sciences in S F*. New York: Delacorte, 1966, pp. 117–135. Damon Knight, ed. *Toward Infinity*. New York: Simon & Schuster, 1968, pp. 194–216.

4

1942

F "Christmas on Ganymede," *Startling Stories*, VII (January), 83–92.

 Early Asimov, 1972

 Kendell F. Crossen, ed. *Adventures in Tomorrow*. New York: Greenberg, 1951, pp. 110–126.

F "Robot AL 76 Goes Astray," *Amazing*, XVI (February), 218–

 The Rest of the Robots, 1964, pp. 3–16.

 Leo Margulies & Oscar J. Friend, eds., *My Best Science Fiction Story*. New York: Merlin, 1949, pp. 3–19.

F "Runaround," *Astounding*, XXIX (March), 94–103.

 I, Robot, 1950, pp. 41–62. Excerpt, *Opus 100*, 1969, pp. 63–64.

 Sam Moskowitz, ed. *The Coming of the Robots*. New York: Collier, 1963, pp. 99–127.

F "Time Pussy" [pseud. George E. Dale], *Astounding*, XXIX (April), 113–114.

 Early Asimov, 1972

F "Foundation," *Astounding*, XXIX (May), 38–52.

 Part I of *Foundation*, 1951.

F "Black Friar of the Flame," *Planet*, I (Spring), 2–27.

 Early Asimov, 1972

F "Bridle and Saddle," *Astounding*, XXIX (June), 9–30.

 Part II of *Foundation*, 1951.

 Martin Greenberg, ed. *Men Against the Stars*. New York: Gnome, 1950, pp. 281–334.

F "Victory Unintentional," *Super Science Stories*, IV (August), 86–99.

 The Rest of the Robots, 1964, pp. 17–37.

 Orson Welles, ed. *Invasion from Mars*. New York: Dell, 1949.

 Milton A. Lesser, ed. *Looking Forward*. New York: Beechhurst, 1953, pp. 230–250.

F "The Hazing," *Thrilling Wonder Stories*, XXIII (October), 89–97, 129.
  Early Asimov, 1972

F "The Imaginary," *Super Science Stories*, IV (November), 74–85.
  Early Asimov, 1972

1943

F "Death Sentence," *Astounding*, XXXII (November), 32–47.
  Early Asimov, 1972
  August W. Derleth, ed. *The Outer Reaches*. New York: Pellegrini & Cudahy, 1950, pp. 31–51.

1944

F "Catch that Rabbit," *Astounding*, XXXII (February), 159–178.
  I, Robot, 1950, pp. 85–110.

F "The Big and the Little," *Astounding*, XXXIII (August), 7–54.
  Part III of *Foundation*, 1951.

F "The Wedge," *Astounding*, XXXIV (October), 64–79.
  Part IV of *Foundation*, 1951.

1945

F "Blind Alley," *Astounding*, XXXV (March), 139–157.
  Early Asimov, 1972
  Groff Conklin, ed. *The Best of Science Fiction*. New York: Crown, 1946, pp. 622–640. Groff Conklin, ed. *Great Stories of Space Travel*. New York: Grosset & Dunlap, 1963, pp. 180–207.

F "Dead Hand," *Astounding*, XXXV (April), 6–60.
  Part I of *Foundation and Empire*, 1952. Excerpt, *Opus 100*, 1969, pp. 243–248.

F "Paradoxical Escape," *Astounding*, XXXV (May), 79–98.
I, Robot, 1950, pp. 167–194, under title "Escape."

F "The Mule" *Astounding*, XXXVI (August), 7–53, 139–144.
Part II of *Foundation and Empire*, 1952.

1946

F "Evidence," *Astounding*, XXXVIII (September), 121–140.
I, Robot, 1950, pp. 195–224.
William F. Nolan, ed. *The Pseudo-People*. New York: Harper &
Row, 1965, pp. 79–102.

1947

F "Little Lost Robot," *Astounding*, XXXIX (March), 120–132.
I, Robot, 1950, pp. 133–166.
Robert Montgomery, ed. [E. Crispin, pseud.] *Best S F #2*. London:
Faber & Faber, 1956, pp. 102–128. Robert Montgomery, ed.
[E. Crispin, pseud.] *The Stars and Under*. London: Faber & Faber,
1968, pp. 72–108.

1948

F "Now You See It . . ." *Astounding*, XL (January), 7–61.
Part I of *Second Foundation*, 1953.

F "The Endochronic Properties of Resublimated Thiotimoline,"
Astounding, XLI (March), 120–125.
Only a Trillion, 1958, as Part I of "The Marvellous Properties of
Thiotimoline," pp. 159–177. *Early Asimov*, 1972

F "No Connection," *Astounding*, XLI (June), 72–87.
Early Asimov, 1972
Everett F. Bleiler & T. E. Dikty, eds. *Best Science Fiction Stories:
1949*. New York: Fell, 1949, pp. 226–249. Everett F. Bleiler &
T. E. Dikty, eds. *Science Fiction Omnibus*. Garden City, N.Y.:
Doubleday, 1952, pp. 226–249.

1949

F "Red Queen's Race," *Astounding,* XLII (January), 65–86.
  Early Asimov, 1972
  Fletcher Pratt, ed. *World of Wonder.* New York: Twayne, 1951,
  pp. 68–94.

F "Mother Earth," *Astounding,* XLIII (May), 59–92.
  Early Asimov, 1972
  Martin Greenberg, ed. *Journey to Infinity.* New York: Gnome,
  1951, pp. 159–195. Leo Margulies, ed. *Three From Out There.*
  Greenwich, Conn.: Fawcett, 1959, pp. 7–46.

F ". . . And Now You Don't," *Astounding,* XLIV, Part one
  (November), 5–40; Part two (December), 120–161;
  Part three (January 1950), 111–152.
  Part II of *Second Foundation,* 1953.

1950

F *I, Robot.* New York: Gnome. London: Grayson, 1952. New
  York American Library, 1956. Toronto, Doubleday, 1963.
  London: Dobson, 1967. New York: Fawcett Crest, 1970.
  Excerpt, *Opus 100,* 1969, p. 65.

F *Pebble in the Sky.* Garden City, N.Y., Doubleday. Galaxy
  Novel ♯ 14, 1953. New York: Bantam, 1957. *Triangle,*
  1961, pp. 173–346. London: Sidgwick & Jackson, 1968.
  New York: Fawcett Crest, 1971.

"The kinetics of the reaction inactivation of tyrosinase during
its catalysis of the aerobic oxidation of catechol" [Abstract
of Dr. Asimov's Ph.D. thesis, Columbia University, 1948],
Journal of the American Chemical Society, LXXII, 820.
Excerpt from the thesis, *Opus 100,* 1969, pp. 185–187.

F "The Little Man on the Subway," *Fantasy Book*, I, no.6 (n.d.), 4–19. In collaboration with Frederik Pohl, under pseud. James MacCreigh.
  Early Asimov, 1972
  Garrett Ford, ed. *Science and Sorcery*. Los Angeles: Fantasy Publications, 1951, pp. 61–78.

F "Evitable Conflict," *Astounding*, XLV (June), 48–68.
  I, Robot, 1950, pp. 225–253.

F "Legal Rites," *Weird Tales*, XLII (September), 8–25. In collaboration with Frederik Pohl, under the pseud. James McCreagh.
  Early Asimov, 1972
  Kurt Singer, ed. *Weird Tales of the Supernatural*. London: W. H. Allen, 1966, pp. 86–112 [No copyright acknowledgement].

F "Darwinian Pool Room," *Galaxy*, I (October), 152–160.

F "Day of the Hunters," *Future*, I (November), 74–79.

F "Misbegotten Missionary," *Galaxy*, I (November), 34–47.
  Nightfall, 1969, pp. 38–52, under the title "Green Patches."
  Robert A. Heinlein, ed. *Tomorrow, the Stars*. Garden City, N.Y.: Doubleday, 1952, pp. 183–199. Groff Conklin, ed. *Giants Unleashed*. New York: Grosset & Dunlap, 1965, pp. 125–161. Robert Hoskins, ed. *First Step Outward*. New York: Dell, 1969

1951

F *Foundation*. New York: Gnome. New York: Ace, 1956, 1963, under the title *The Thousand Year Plan*. Garden City, N.Y.: Doubleday, 1963. New York: Avon, 1966, 1969, 1970.
  Foundation Trilogy, 1961. *An Isaac Asimov Omnibus*, 1966.

F *The Stars, Like Dust*. *See* "Tyrann," January 1951.

F "In a Good Cause," in *New Tales of Space and Time.*
Robert J. Healy, ed. New York: Holt, pp. 19–48.
Nightfall, 1969, pp. 166–190.

F "Tyrann," *Galaxy*, I: Part one (January), 4–65; Part two
(February), 108–159; Part three (March), 98–160.
The Stars, Like Dust. Garden City, N.Y.: Doubleday. New York:
Ace, 1954, under the title *The Rebellious Stars.* Bound with
An Earth Gone Mad, R. D. Aycock [Dr. Asimov's comment:
"ludicrously cut without my permission"]. New York: Lancer,
1970. *Triangle*, 1961, pp. 347–516.

"Other Worlds to Conquer," *The Writer*, LXIV (May),
148–151.
A. S. Burack, ed. *Writer's Handbook.* Boston: The Writer, Inc.,
1959, pp. 321–327 [also appeared in subsequent editions through
1963].

F "Satisfaction Guaranteed," *Amazing*, XXV (April), 52–63.
Fantastic Stories, XV (July 1966), 114–128.
Earth Is Room Enough, 1957, pp. 114–127. *The Rest of the Robots*,
1964, pp. 67–82.
Roger Elwood, ed. *The Invasion of the Robots.* New York:
Paperback Library, 1965, pp. 9–21.

F "Breeds there a Man . . . ?" *Astounding*, XLVII (June),
73–103.
Through a Glass, Clearly, 1967. *Nightfall*, 1969, pp. 94–128.
August W. Derleth, ed. *Beachheads in Space.* New York:
Pellegrini & Cudahy, 1952, pp. 169–203.

F "Hostess," *Galaxy*, II (May), 86–123.
Nightfall, 1969, pp. 54–92.
H. L. Gold, ed. *Galaxy Reader of Science Fiction.* New York:
Crown, 1952, pp. 305–335.

F "C-Chute," *Galaxy*, III (October), 3–41.

Through a Glass, Clearly, 1967. *Nightfall*, 1969, pp. 130–164.
Frederik Pohl, ed. *Shadow of Tomorrow*. Garden City, N.Y.:
Doubleday, 1953, pp. 58–97. H. L. Gold, ed. *Second Galaxy
of Science Fiction*. Garden City, N.Y.: Doubleday, 1954,
pp. 97–129.

F "Shah Guido G," *Marvel*, III (November), 27–33.

F "The Fun They Had," *Boys and Girls Page* [syndicated
newspaper feature], NEA Service, December 1.

F&SF, VI (February 1954), 125–127.

Earth Is Room Enough, 1957, pp. 146–148. Isaac Asimov & Groff
Conklin, eds. *Fifty Short Science Fiction Tales*. New York:
Collier, 1963, pp. 25–28.

Groff Conklin, ed. *Operation Future*. New York: Doubleday, 1955,
pp. 353–356. Richard L. Laughlin & Lillian M. Popp, eds.
Journey in S F [a textbook]. New York: Globe, 1961, pp. 567–574.
Thomas W. Boardman, ed. *Connoisseur's S F*. Baltimore Penguin,
1964, pp. 146–149.

1952

F *The Currents of Space. See* "The Currents of Space,"
October 1952.

F *David Starr, Space Ranger.* [Pseud. Paul French] Garden
City, N.Y.: Doubleday. New York: New American
Library/Signet, 1972.

F *Foundation and Empire.* New York: Gnome. New York:
Ace, 1955, under the title *The Man Who Upset the Universe*.
Garden City, N.Y.: Doubleday, 1963. New York:
Avon, 1966, 1970.

Biochemistry and Human Metabolism. With B. S. Walker
and W.C. Boyd. Baltimore: Williams & Wilkins.

Excerpt, *Opus 100*, 1969, pp. 156–157.

"Origin and Evolution of Man," *Evolution*, VI (March), 134–136.

F "Youth," *Space Science Fiction*, I (May)
  The Martian Way and Other Stories, 1955, pp. 72–109.

F "What If . . ." *Fantastic*, I (Summer), 106–118.
  Nightfall, 1969, pp. 191–204.
  Groff Conklin, ed. *S F Adventures in Dimension*. New York: Vanguard, 1953, pp. 235–248. Groff Conklin, ed. *Great S F by Scientists*. New York: Collier, 1962, pp. 17–32.

F "The Currents of Space," *Astounding*, L: Part one (October), 7–68; Part two (November), 101–151; Part three (December), 104–163.
  The Currents of Space. Garden City, N.Y.: Doubleday. New York: New American Library, 1953. London: Boardman, 1955. New York: Lancer, 1968. Greenwich, Conn.: Fawcett, 1971. *Triangle*, 1961, pp. 1–172.

F "The Deep," *Galaxy*, V (November), 139–160.
  The Martian Way, 1955, pp. 110–136.

F "The Martian Way," *Galaxy*, V (December), 4–49.
  The Martian Way, 1955, pp. 13–71. Excerpt, *Opus 100*, 1969, pp. 33–38.
  Damon Knight, ed. *Worlds to Come*. New York: Fawcett, 1968, pp. 141–212.

1953

F *Lucky Starr and the Pirates of the Asteroids*. [Pseud. Paul French] Garden City, N.Y.: Doubleday. New York: New American Library/Signet, 1972.

F *Second Foundation*. New York: Gnome. New York: Avon, 1958, 1964, 1970. Garden City, N.Y.: Doubleday, 1963.
  Foundation Trilogy, 1961. *An Isaac Asimov Omnibus*, 1966.

F "Nobody Here But . . ." in *Star S.F. Stories*, Frederik Pohl,
ed. Boston: Houghton Mifflin, 143–154.

"Social Science Fiction," in *Modern Science Fiction*,
Reginald Bretnor, ed. New York: Coward-McCann,
pp. 157–196.

F "Button, Button," *Startling Stories*, XXVIII (January), 74–82.
Groff Conklin, ed. *13 Above the Night*. New York: Dell, 1969,
pp. 189–204.

F "The Monkey's Fingers," *Startling Stories*, XXIX (February),
77–83.

F "Sally," *Fantastic*, I (May–June), 34–50, 162.
Nightfall, 1969, pp. 206-223.
E. Abell, ed. *American Accent*. New York: Ballantine, 1954,
pp. 124–143.

F "Flies," *F&SF*, IV (June), 17–22.
Nightfall, 1969, pp. 225-231.
Groff Conklin, ed. *S F Terror Tales*. New York: Gnome, 1955,
pp. 115–123.

F "Kid Stuff," *Beyond*, I (September), 121–133.
Earth Is Room Enough, 1957, pp. 80–92.

F "Belief," *Astounding*, LII (October), 71–99.
Through a Glass, Clearly, 1967,
Judith Merrill, ed. *Beyond the Barriers of Space and Time*. New
York: Random House, 1954, pp. 153–184. John W. Campbell, ed.
Prologue to Analog: Analog Science Fact and Science Fiction.
Garden City, N.Y.: Doubleday, 1962, pp. 19–58.

F "The Caves of Steel," *Galaxy*, VII: Part One (October), 4–66;
Part Two (November), 98–159; Part Three (December),
108–159.
The Caves of Steel. Garden City, N.Y.: Doubleday, 1954. New

York: New American Library, 1955. New York: Pyramid, 1962.
The Rest of the Robots, 1964, pp. 165–362.

Excerpts in *The Sociology of the Possible*, Richard Ofshe, ed.
Englewood Cliffs, N.J.: Prentice-Hall, 1970, pp. 220–234.

F "The Micropsychiatric Applications of Thiotimoline,"
Astounding, LII (December), 107–116.

Only a Trillion, 1957, as Part Two of "The Marvelous Properties
of Thiotimoline," pp. 159–177.

"Natural Occurrence of Short-Lived Radio-Isotopes," *J.C.E.*,
XXX (December), 616–618.

F "Everest," *Universe Science Fiction*, III (December), 30–33.

1954

F *The Caves of Steel. See* "The Caves of Steel," October 1953.

The Chemicals of Life. New York: Abelard-Schuman.
London: Bell, 1956. New York: New American Library,
1963. New York: Signet, 1970.

Excerpt, *Sci Di*, XXXVII (September 1955), 13–17, under the
title "Protein, Key to Life."
Excerpt, *Opus 100*, 1969, pp. 159-163.

F *Lucky Starr and the Oceans of Venus*. [Pseud. Paul French]
Garden City, N.Y.: Doubleday. New York: New American
Library/Signet, 1972.

Excerpt, *Opus 100*, 1969, pp. 30–32.

F *The Rebellious Stars. See The Stars, Like Dust*, 1951.

F "It's Such a Beautiful Day," *Star S. F. Stories No. 3*, Frederik
Pohl, ed. Boston: Houghton Mifflin, pp. 1–25.

Through a Glass, Clearly, 1967
John Standler, ed. *Eco-Fiction*. New York: Washington Square
Press, 1971, pp. 183–206.

F "The Pause," in *Time to Come: S F Stories of Tomorrow*, August W. Derleth, ed. New York: Farrar, Straus, pp. 41–59.

"The Foundation of S F Success" [poem], *F&SF*, VI (January), 69.
Earth Is Room Enough, 1957, pp. 56–57.
Anthony Boucher and J. F. McComas, eds. *Best From Fantasy and Science Fiction, Fourth Series*. Boston: Little, Brown, 1955, pp. 249–250.

"Relative Contributions of Various Elements to the Earth's Radioactivity," *J.C.E.*, XXXI (January), 24–25.

"Elementary Composition of the Earth's Crust," *J.C.E.*, XXXI (February), 70–72.

F "Sucker Bait," *Astounding*: Part One, LII (February), 8–38; Part Two, LIII (March), 111–139.
The Martian Way, 1955, pp. 137–222.

"Potentialities of Protein Isomerism," *J.C.E.*, XXXI (March), 125–127.

F "Immortal Bard," *Universe*, No. 5 (May), 97–99.
Earth Is Room Enough, 1957, pp. 162–164.

F "Let's Not," *Graduate Journal* [Boston University], III (December), 53–54.
Martin Greenberg, ed. *All About the Future*. New York: Gnome, 1955, pp. 34–26.

1955

F *The End of Eternity*. Garden City, N.Y.: Doubleday. New York: New American Library, 1958. New York: Lancer, 1963, 1966, 1968. Garden City, N.Y.: Doubleday, 1966. Greenwich, Conn.: Fawcett Crest, 1971.

F *The Man Who Upset the Universe. See Foundation and Empire*, 1952.

F *The Martian Way, and Other Stories*. Garden City, N.Y.: Doubleday. New York: New American Library, 1957. London: Dobson, 1964. Greenwich, Conn.: Fawcett Crest, 1969, 1971.

Races and People. With William C. Boyd. New York: Abelard-Schuman. Canada: Nelson, 1955. New York: Abelard-Schuman, 1958. New York: Random House, 1964.

F "The Singing Bell," *F&SF*, VIII (January), 97–110.
Asimov's Mysteries, 1968, pp. 1–17.
Anthony Boucher, ed. *Best from Fantasy and Science Fiction, 5th Series*. Garden City, N.Y.: Doubleday, 1956, pp. 226–244.

"Hemoglobin and the Universe," *Astounding*, LIV (February), 129–140.
Only a Trillion, 1957, pp. 38–51.

"Radioactivity of the Human Body," *J.C.E.*, XXXII (February), 84–85.

F "Risk," *Astounding*, LV (May), 60–82.
The Rest of the Robots, 1964, pp. 83–110.

"The Sound of Panting," *Astounding*, LV (June), 104–113.
Only a Trillion, 1957, pp. 145–155. Excerpt, *Opus 100*, 1969, pp. 152–154.

F "Last Trump," *Fantastic Universe*, III (June), 41–54.
Earth Is Room Enough, 1957, pp. 130–145.

F "Franchise," *If*, V (August), 2–15.
Earth Is Room Enough, 1957, pp. 58–73.
James L. Quinn & Eve Wulff, eds. *The First World of IF*. Kingston, N.Y.: Quinn Publications, 1957. Roger Elwood & Sam Moskowitz, eds. *Alien Earth and Other Stories*. New York:

16

McFadden, 1969, pp. 193–208. Richard Ofshe, ed. *The Sociology of the Possible*. Englewood Cliffs, N.J.: Prentice-Hall, 1970, pp. 162–173.

"Victory on Paper," *Astounding*, LVI (September), 112–123.
Only a Trillion, 1958, pp. 52–66.

F "The Talking Stone," *F&SF*, IX (October), 107–123.
Asimov's Mysteries, 1968, pp. 18–37.
Miriam A. DeFord, ed. *Space, Time and Crime*. New York: Mercury, 1964, pp. 43–59.

F "Dreamworld," *F&SF*, IX (November), 127.
Opus 100, 1969, pp. 290–291.
Anthony Boucher, ed. *The Best From Fantasy and Science Fiction, 5th Series*. Garden City, N.Y.: Doubleday, 1956, pp. 144–145.

F "Dreaming Is a Private Thing," *F&SF*, IX (December), 53–66.
Earth Is Room Enough, 1957, pp. 177–192.
Judith Merril, ed. *S-F: The Year's Greatest Science Fiction and Fantasy*. New York: Gnome, 1956, pp. 270–287. Judith Merril, ed. *S-F: The Best of the Best*. New York: Delacorte, 1967, pp. 398–414.

"Composition of the Atmosphere," *J.C.E.*, XXXII (December), 633–634.

F "The Portable Star," *Thrilling Wonder Stories*, XLIV (Winter), 54–64.

1956

Chemistry and Human Health. With B. S. Walker and M. K. Nicholas. New York: McGraw-Hill.

Inside the Atom. New York: Abelard-Schuman. Revised edition, 1958. Second edition, 1959. Revised edition, 1960. Second revised edition, 1961. Third revised edition, 1966.

F *Lucky Starr and the Big Sun of Mercury*. [Pseud. Paul French]
Garden City, N.Y.: Doubleday. New York: New
American Library/Signet, 1972.

F *The Thousand Year Plan. See Foundation*, 1951.

F "Each an Explorer," Future, xxx (n.d.)
Judith Merril, ed. *S F '57: The Year's Greatest S F & Fantasy*.
New York: Gnome, 1957.

F "The Message," *F&SF*, x (February), 120–121.
Earth Is Room Enough, 1957, pp. 112–113.

"Elementary composition of the earth," *J.C.E.*, xxx
(February), 67.

Letter [in reply to Randall Garrett], *Original*, vi
(March), 132.

F "Dead Past," *Astounding*, lvii (April), 6–46.
Earth Is Room Enough, 1957, pp. 11–15.

"The Abnormality of Being Normal," *Astounding*, lvii
(May), 121–131.
Only a Trillion, 1957, pp. 67–79.

F "Hell-fire," *Fantastic Universe*, v (May), 97–98.
Earth Is Room Enough, 1957, pp. 128–129.

F "Living Space," *Original Stories*, vi (May), 3–17.
Earth Is Room Enough, 1957, pp. 98–111.
Robert Silverberg, ed. *Worlds of Maybe*. New York: Thomas
Nelson, 1970, pp. 152–172.

F "Brazen Locked Room," *F&SF*, xi (June), 110–114.
Earth Is Room Enough, 1957, pp. 74–79, under the title "Gimmicks
Three."
Basil Davenport, ed. *Deals With the Devil*. New York: Dodd,
Mead, 1958, pp. 1–8. J. Francis McComas, ed. *Special Wonder:
The Anthony Boucher Memorial Anthology of Fantasy and Science
Fiction*. New York: Random House, 1970, pp. 12–17.

18

F "Death of a Honey-Blonde," *Saint Detective Stories*, V (June), 110–125.
Asimov's Mysteries, 1968, pp. 38–53, under the title "What's in a Name?"

F "The Dying Night," *F&SF*, XI (July), 3–24.
Nine Tomorrows, 1959, pp. 86–112. *Asimov's Mysteries*, 1968, pp. 54–79.

"The By-Product of Science Fiction," *Chemical and Engineering News*, XXXIV (August), 3882–3886.
Is Anyone There? 1967, pp. 291–297, under the title "The Cult of Ignorance."

F "Someday," *Infinity*, I (August), 26–35.
Earth Is Room Enough, 1957, pp. 165–173.
Damon Knight, ed. *The Metal Smile*. New York: Belmont, 1968, pp. 134–144. Harry Harrison, ed. *Worlds of Wonder*. Garden City, New York: Doubleday, 1969, pp. 276–285.
See also "The Story Machine," 1958.

"S-F Market Still Healthy" [letter to the editor], *The Writer*, LXIX (August), 218.

F "Pâté de Foie Gras," *Astounding*, LVIII (September), 103–117.
Only a Trillion, 1957, pp. 178–195. *Asimov's Mysteries*, 1968, pp. 80–95.

F "The Naked Sun," *Astounding*, LVIII, Part One (October), 8–62; Part Two (November), 96–151; Part Three (December), 89–146.
The Naked Sun. Garden City, N.Y.: Doubleday, 1957. London: M. Joseph, 1958. New York: Bantam, 1958. New York: Lancer, 1964, 1969.
The Rest of the Robots, 1964, pp. 364–554.

F "First Law," *Fantastic Universe*, VI (October), 29–31.
   The Rest of the Robots, 1964, pp. 41–46.
   Hans Santesson, ed. *The Fantastic Universe Omnibus*. Englewood
   Cliffs, N.J., Prentice-Hall, 1960, pp. 1–4.

F "Watery Place," *Satellite*, I (October), 86–89.
   Earth Is Room Enough, 1957, pp. 93–97.

F "The Last Question," *Science Fiction Quarterly*, IV
   (November), 7–15.
   Nine Tomorrows, 1959, pp. 177–190. *Opus 100*, 1969, pp. 69–84.

   "How to Succeed at Science Fiction Without Really Trying,"
   Original, VII (November), 110–111.

   "Names! Names! Names!" *Astounding*, LVIII (December),
   69–88.

F "Jokester," *Infinity*, I (December), 39–51.
   Earth Is Room Enough, 1957, pp. 149–161.
   Brian Aldiss, ed. *More Penguin S F*. London: Penguin, 1963.

1957

   Building Blocks of the Universe. New York: Abelard-
   Schuman. Revised edition, 1961. Eau Claire, Wisc.: Hale,
   1965. New York: Lancer, 1966.

F *Earth Is Room Enough: Science Fiction Tales of Our Own
   Planet*. Garden City, N.Y.: Doubleday. New York:
   Bantam, 1959. Greenwich, Conn.: Fawcett World, 1970

F *Lucky Starr and the Moons of Jupiter*. [Pseud. Paul French]
   Garden City, N.Y.: Doubleday. New York: New American
   Library/Signet, 1972.
   Excerpt, *Opus 100*, 1969, pp. 8–15.

F *The Naked Sun. See* "The Naked Sun," October 1956.

20

Only a Trillion. New York: Abelard-Schuman. New York:
Collier, 1963, under the title *Marvels of Science*.
 Excerpt, Opus 100, 1969, pp. 138–140.

"The Atoms That Vanish," in *Only a Trillion*, 1957,
pp. 11–24.

"The Explosions Within Us," in *Only a Trillion*, 1957,
25–37.

F "Male Strikebreaker," Original, VII (January), 39–52.
 Nightfall and Other Stories, 1969, pp. 268–281, under the title
 "Strikebreaker."
 Groff Conklin, ed. *17 x Infinity*. New York: Dell, 1963, pp. 20–34,
 under the title "Strikebreaker."

F "Dust of Death," *Venture*, V (January), 83–93.
 Asimov's Mysteries, 1968, pp. 96–107.
 Brett Halliday, ed. *Big Time Mysteries*. New York: Mystery
 Writers of America, Inc., 1958.

F "Let's Get Together," *Infinity*, II (February), 64–80.
 The Rest of the Robots, 1964, pp. 47–64.
 Judith Merril, ed. *S F '58: The Year's Greatest S F and Fantasy*.
 Garden City, N.Y.: Doubleday, 1958, pp. 58–76.

"The Big Number," *Science World*, I (February), 10–11.

"Planets Have an Air About Them," *Astounding*, LIX
(March), 91–104.
 Only a Trillion, 1957, pp. 80–96.

"A Pinch of Life," *Science World*, I (March 5), 8–9.
 Is Anyone There? 1967, pp. 66–70.

"The Ocean Mine," *Science World*, I (March 19), 12–14.
 Is Anyone There? 1967, pp. 115–120.

"The Unblind Workings of Chance," *Astounding*, LIX (April), 85–98.
Only a Trillion, 1957, pp. 97–112.

"The Trapping of the Sun," *Astounding*, LIX (May), 80–95.
Only a Trillion, 1957, pp. 113–131.

Letter to the editor, *Bulletin of Atomic Scientists*, LXIII (May), inside back cover.

"Author's Ordeal" [poem], *Science Fiction Quarterly*, V (May), 34–36.
Earth Is Room Enough, 1957, pp. 174–176.

"Not by Bread Alone," *Science World*, I (May 14), 10–11.

F "Does a Bee Care?" *If*, VII (June), 69–73.
Roger Elwood and Sam Moskowitz, eds. *Other Worlds, Other Times*. New York: McFadden-Bartell, 1969, pp. 119–125.

F "Blank!" *Infinity*, II (June), 88–92.

F "A Woman's Heart," *Satellite*, I (June), 123–124.

"Sometimes You're Right," *Writer*, LXX (June), 14–16.

F "Profession," *Astounding*, LIX (July), 8–56.
Nine Tomorrows, 1959, pp. 16–74.
Excerpts in *The Sociology of the Possible*, Richard Ofshe, ed. Englewood Cliffs, N.J.: Prentice-Hall, 1970, pp. 130–145.
[Excerpted in such a way that the entire point of the original story is lost.]

"The Sea-Urchin and We," *Astounding*, LIX (July), 96–106.
Only a Trillion, 1957, pp. 132–144.

"Tale of the Pioneer" [poem], *Future*, No. 33 (Summer), 76–78.

F "A Loint of Paw," *F&SF*, XIII (August), 130.
  Asimov's Mysteries, 1968, 108-109.
  Anthony Boucher, ed. *Best from Fantasy and Science Fiction, 7th series*. Garden City, N.Y.: Doubleday, 1958, pp. 182–183.

"Axioms for Everybody," *Science Fiction Quarterly*, V (August), 18–24.

"The Unrare Earths," *Fantastic Universe*, VIII (September), 87–91.

"Overflowing the Periodic Table," *Astounding*, LX (October), 87–95.

F "Ideas Die Hard," *Galaxy*, XIV (October), 126–144.
  H. L. Gold, ed. *Third Galaxy Reader*. Garden City, N.Y.: Doubleday, 1958, pp. 121–141. Hal Clement, ed. *First Flights to the Moon*. Garden City, N.Y.: Doubleday, 1970, pp. 75–96.

"The Clock Paradox," *Science Fiction Quarterly*, V (November), 72–73.

F "I'm in Marsport Without Hilda," *Venture*, I (November), 67–78.
  Nine Tomorrows, 1959, pp. 113–126. *Asimov's Mysteries*, 1968, pp. 110–124.

"The Whenabouts of Radioactivity," *Astounding*, LX (December), 132–147.

"I Feel It in My Bones," *F&SF*, XIII (December), 5–18.

F "Insert Knob A in Hole B," *F&SF*, XIII (December), 91.
  Nightfall, 1969, pp. 282–283.

F "Galley Slave," *Galaxy*, XV (December), 8–41.
  The Rest of the Robots, 1964, pp. 127–162.
  Frederik Pohl, ed. *Time Waits for Winthrop, and Four Other Short Novels from Galaxy*. Garden City, N.Y.: Doubleday, 1962, pp. 297–336. Groff Conklin, ed. *Six Great Short S F Novels*. New York: Dell, 1960, pp. 11–50.

"Escape Into Reality," *The Humanist*, XVII (November–December), 326–332.
> *Is Anyone There?* 1967, pp. 283–290.

F "The Gentle Vultures," *Super Science Fiction*, II (December), 2–20.
> *Nine Tomorrows*, 1959, pp. 127–143.
> Robert Silverberg, ed. *Earthmen and Strangers*. New York: Duell, Sloan & Pearce, 1966, pp. 117–137.

1958

F *The Death Dealers*. New York: Avon, 1958. New York: Walker, 1958, under the title *A Whiff of Death*. New York: Lancer, 1969.

F *Lucky Starr and the Rings of Saturn*. [Pseud. Paul French] Garden City, N.Y.: Doubleday. New York: New American Library/Signet, 1972.

The World of Carbon. New York: Abelard-Schuman. Revised edition, New York: Collier, 1962.

The World of Nitrogen. New York: Abelard-Schuman. Revised edition, New York: Collier, 1962.

F "Lenny," *Infinity*, III (January), 54–67.
> *The Rest of the Robots*, 1964, pp. 111–126.
> Frederik Pohl, ed. *The Expert Dreamers*. New York: Avon, 1962, pp. 62–79.

"Oh, That Lost Sense of Wonder" [poem], *Original*, VII (January), 103.

F "S, as in Zebatinsky," *Star Science Fiction*, I (January), 33–47.
> *Nine Tomorrows*, 1959, pp. 161–176, under the title "Spell My Name With an S."

24

"Fecundity Limited," *Venture*, II (January), 37–40.
Is Anyone There? 1967, pp. 230–233.

"I Just Make Them Up, See!" [poem], *F&SF*, XIV
(February), 129–130.
Nine Tomorrows, 1959, pp. 13–15.

F "Silly Asses," *Future*, XXXV (February), 114.

F "The Feeling of Power," *If*, VIII (February), 4–11, 115.
Nine Tomorrows, 1959, pp. 75–85. *Opus 100*, 1969, pp. 106–117.
Clifton Fadiman, ed. *The Mathematical Magpie*. New York:
Simon & Schuster, 1962, pp. 3–14. Kingsley Amis & Robert
Conquest, eds. *Spectrum II*. New York: Harcourt, Brace & World,
1963, pp. 165–174. Robert Hoskins, ed. *The Stars Around Us*.
New York: New American Library, 1970, pp. 129–138.

"Story Machine," *Plays*, XVII (February), 13–23.
Plays, XXIX (May 1970), 25–34. [An adaptation of "Someday,"
August 1956.]

"The Littlest," *Original*, VIII (March), 77–91.

"The Atmosphere of the Moon," *Venture*, II (March), 23–26.
Is Anyone There? 1967, pp. 133–135.

F "All the Troubles of the World," *Super Science Fiction*,
II (April), 34–53.
Nine Tomorrows, 1959, pp. 144–160.

"The Big Bang," *Venture*, II (May), 19–22.

F "Buy Jupiter," *Venture*, II (May), 84–97.

"Point of View," *Future*, XXXV *(June)*, 57–63.

F "Up-to-Date Sorcerer," *F&SF*, XV (July), 72–84.
Nightfall, 1969, pp. 285–298.
Anthony Boucher, ed. *The Best from Fantasy and Science Fiction,
8th Series*. Garden City, N.Y.: Doubleday, 1959, pp. 55–70.

"The Clash of Cymbals," *Venture*, II (July), 50–54.

"Point of View: Mercury," *Future*, XXXV (August), 51–68.

Book reviews of science books for children, *Hornbook*, XXXIV (August), 274, 277. First in a series.

F "Lastborn," *Galaxy*, XVI (September), 6–44.
   Under the title "The Ugly Little Boy": *Nine Tomorrows*, 1959, pp. 191–233; *Tomorrow's Children*, 1966, pp. 389–431.
   R. P. Mills, ed. *The Worlds of Science Fiction*. New York: Dial, 1963, pp. 293-339. Damon Knight, ed. *Dimension X*. New York: Simon & Schuster, 1970, pp. 303–350.

"Breakthroughs in Science: Archimedes," *Senior Scholastic*, LXXIII (September 12), 24–25; "Gutenberg," (September 19), 14–15. First in a series.
   Printed in book form, *Breakthroughs in Science*, 1960.

"It's All How You Look at It" [poem], *Future*, XXXIX (October), 50.
   Judith Merril, ed. *S F '59: The Year's Greatest Science Fiction and Fantasy*. Hicksville, N.Y.: Gnome, 1959, pp. 239–240, as part of an original article, "The Thunder-Thieves."

Book reviews, *Hornbook*, XXXIV (October), 392–396.

"Breakthroughs in Science," *Senior Scholastic*, LXXIII: "Copernicus" (October 3), 18–19; "William Harvey" (October 10), 19; "Galileo" (October 24), 16–17; "Van Leeuwenhoek" (October 31), 13.

"Our Lonely Planet," *Astounding*, LXII (November), 127–137.
   Fact and Fancy, 1962, pp. 167–182.

"The Dust of Ages," *F&SF*, XV (November), 35–38.
   First in a series of articles on science.
   Sci Di, XLV (January 1959), 33–35, under the title "14 Million Tons of Dust Per Year."

"Breakthroughs in Science," *Senior Scholastic*, LXXIII:
"Sir Isaac Newton" (November 7), 14–15; "James Watt"
(November 14), 15; "Lavoisier" (November 21), 16–17.

"Catching Up With Newton," *F&SF*, xv (December),
31–44.
Fact and Fancy, 1962, pp. 63-78.

Book reviews, *Hornbook*, XXXIV (December), 483–487.

"Breakthroughs in Science," *Senior Scholastic*, LXXIII:
"Faraday" (December 5), 22, 24; "James Henry"
(December 12), 14–15.

1959

The Clock We Live On. New York: Abelard-Schuman.
New revised edition, New York: Collier, 1962. Revised
edition, New York: Abelard-Schuman, 1965.
Eau Claire, Wisc.: Hale, 1968.

F *Nine Tomorrows*: *Tales of the Near Future*. Garden City,
N.Y.: Doubleday. New York: Bantam, 1961. London:
Dobson, 1963. Greenwich, Conn.: Fawcett Crest,
1969. Garden City, N.Y.: Doubleday, 1970.

The Realm of Numbers. Boston: Houghton Mifflin. Toronto:
T. Allen, 1959. London: Gollancz, 1963. Eau Claire,
Wisc.: Hale, 1965. Greenwich, Conn.: Fawcett, 1967, 1971.
Excerpt, *Opus 100*, 1969, pp. 90–93.

Words of Science, and the History Behind Them. Boston:
Houghton Mifflin. Toronto: T. Allen, 1959. Eau Claire,
Wisc.: Hale, 1964. New York: New American
Library, 1969.
Excerpts, *Sci Di*, XLVI (September 1959), 60–64, under the title
"Tracing Words of Science."
Excerpt, *Opus 100*, 1969, pp. 216–220.

"Rejection Slips," in *Nine Tomorrows*, 1959, pp. 234–236.

"The Thunder-Thieves," in *S F '59: The Year's Greatest Science Fiction and Fantasy*, ed. by Judith Merril. Hicksville, N.Y.: Gnome, 1959, pp. 239–247.

"No More Ice Ages?" *F&SF*, XVI (January), 21–33.
Fact and Fancy, 1962, pp. 31–46.

"Breakthroughs in Science," *Senior Scholastic*, LXXIII:
"Bessemer," (January 9) 19; "Sir Edward Jenner" (January 16), 16–17; "Pasteur," (January 23), 18–19; "Mendel" (January 30), 15.

"Love Those Zeroes," *F&SF*, XVI (February), 26–31.

Book reviews, *Hornbook*, XXXV (February), 50–53.

F "A Statue for Father," *Satellite*, III (February), 33-41.

"Breakthroughs in Science," *Senior Scholastic*, LXXIV:
"W. H. Perkin" (February 13), 14–15; "Roentgen and Becquerel" (February 27), 36–37.

F "Anniversary," *Amazing*, XXXIII (March), 24–37.
Asimov's Mysteries, 1968, pp. 141–156.
Joseph Ross, ed. *The Best of Amazing*. Garden City, N.Y.: Doubleday, 1967, pp. 107-125.

"Nothing," *F&SF*, XVI (March), 16–19.
Sci Di, XLV (May), 13–16, under the title "Is Outer Space Really Empty?"

"Breakthroughs in Science," *Senior Scholastic*, LXXIV:
"Edison" (March 6), 14–15; "Ehrlich" (March 13), 10–11; "Darwin and Wallace" (March 20), 22–23.

"Life's Bottleneck," *F&SF*, XVI (April), 31–40.
Fact and Fancy, 1962, pp. 17–30.

28

F "Unto the Fourth Generation," *F&SF*, XVI (April), 80–86.
   Nightfall, 1969, pp. 299–306.
   Robert Mills, ed. *A Decade of Fantasy and Science Fiction*. Garden
   City, N.Y.: Doubleday, 1960, pp. 183–191.

Book reviews, *Hornbook*, XXXV (April), 140–143.

"Breakthroughs in Science," *Senior Scholastic*, LXXIV: "Marie
and Pierre Curie" (April 3), 50–51; "Albert Einstein"
(April 10), 16–17; "George Washington Carver" (April
17), 11; "Irving Langmuir" (April 24), 21.

"Of Capture and Escape," *F&SF*, XVI (May), 24–36.
   Fact and Fancy, 1962, pp. 79–91.

"Breakthroughs in Science," *Senior Scholastic*, LXXIV:
"Rutherford and Lawrence" (May 1), 12–13; "Robert
Goddard" (May 8), 13.

"The Planet of the Double Sun," *F&SF*, XVI (June), 24–33.
   Fact and Fancy, 1962, pp. 137–149.

Book reviews, *Hornbook*, XXXV (June), 224–227.

"The Unused Stars," *Amazing*, XXXIII (July), 141–145.
   Is Anyone There? 1967, pp. 144–149.

"The Unartificial Elements," *Astounding*, LXIII (July),
58–61.

"Battle of the Eggheads," *F&SF*, XVI (July), 43–52.
   Fact and Fancy, 1962, pp. 251–264.

F "Obituary," *F&SF*, XVII (August), 103–117.
   Asimov's Mysteries, 1968, pp. 157–173.

"The Ultimate Split of the Second," *F&SF*, XVII (August),
25–34.
   View from a Height, 1963, pp. 123–134.
   Excerpt in *The Scientist Speculates*, I. J. Good, ed. New York:
   Basic Books, 1962, pp. 348–350, under the title "The Light-Mile."

"Point of View: The Moon," *Future*, xliv (August), 28–45.

Book reviews, *Hornbook*, xxxv (August), 304–308.

"Earth-Grazers: 'H Bombs' in Space," *Space Age*, (August)
Sci Di, xlvi (November), 77–82.

"Varieties of the Infinite," *F&SF*, xvii (September), 40–49.
Adding a Dimension, 1964, pp. 27–37.

F "Rain, Rain, Go Away," *Fantastic Universe*, xi (September),
4–10.

"The Height of Up," *F&SF*, xvii (October), 61–67.
Sci Di, xlvi (December 1959), 61–67, under the title "Three
Scales of Temperature."
View From a Height, 1963, pp. 165–180.

Book reviews, *Hornbook*, xxxv (October), 394–397.

"C for Celeritas," *F&SF*, xvii (November), 100–109.
Of Time and Space and Other Things, 1965, pp. 146–156.

"Enzymes and Metaphor," *J.C.E.*, xxxvi (November),
535–538.
Is Anyone There? 1967, pp. 56–65.

"Thin Air," *F&SF*, xvii (December), 34–44.
Sci Di, xlvii (March 1960), 36–41, under the title "What We
Know About the Air."
Fact and Fancy, 1962, pp. 57–62.

Book reviews, *Hornbook*, xxxv (December), 491–495.

1960

Breakthroughs in Science. Boston: Houghton Mifflin.
Toronto: T. Allen, 1960. Eau Claire, Wisc.: Hale, 1964.
Englewood Cliffs, N.J.: Scholastic Book Service/Starline,
1971.

The Double Planet. London, New York: Abelard-Schuman. Revised edition, 1966. New York: Pyramid, 1968.

The Intelligent Man's Guide to Science, 2 vols. New York: Basic Books. Vol. II, under the title *The Intelligent Man's Guide to the Biological Sciences.* New York: Pocket Books, 1964. New York: Simon & Schuster, 1970. Vol. I, under the title *The Intelligent Man's Guide to the Physical Sciences.* New York: Pocket Books, 1965. New York: Simon & Schuster, 1970. *The New Intelligent Man's Guide to Science, revised edition,* 1 vol. New York: Basic Books, 1965. [Excerpt, *Opus 100,* 1969, pp. 67–68.] Third Edition. New York: Basic Books, 1972, under the title *Asimov's Guide to Science.*

The Kingdom of the Sun. London, New York: Abelard-Schuman. Revised & enlarged edition, New York: Collier, 1962. Revised edition, New York: Abelard-Schuman, 1963. Eau Claire, Wisc.: Hale, 1965.

The Living River. New York: Abelard-Schuman. Revised edition, New York: Collier, 1961, under the title *The Bloodstream: River of Life.*

The Realm of Measure. Boston: Houghton Mifflin. Toronto: T. Allen, 1960. Greenwich, Conn.: Fawcett, 1967, 1971.

Satellites in Outer Space. New York: Random House. Eau Claire, Wisc.: Hale, 1960. Revised edition, New York: Random House, 1964.

The Wellsprings of Life. New York: Abelard-Schuman. New York: New American Library (Signet), 1961. Excerpt, *Opus 100,* 1969, pp. 192–197.

"Those Crazy Ideas," *F&SF,* xviii (January), 55–64. *Fact and Fancy,* 1962, pp. 223–236.

31

"The Sight of Home," *F&SF*, XVIII (February), 86–94.
  Fact and Fancy, 1962, pp. 195–206.

Book reviews, *Hornbook*, XXXVI (February), 49–54.

"Microdesign for Living," *Astounding*, LXV (March), 104–121.

"The Flickering Yardstick," *F&SF*, XVIII (March), 79–88.
  Excerpt, *Sci Di*, LXVII (May 1960), 53–59.
  Fact and Fancy, 1962, pp. 183–194.

"About Time," *F&SF*, XVIII (April), 85–95.
  Excerpt, *Sci Di*, XLVIII (October 1960), 53–58, under the title "It's About Time for a Metric Calendar."

Book reviews, *Hornbook*, XXXVI (April), 146–149.

"The March of the Phyla," *Astounding*, LXV (May), 83–103.

"A Piece of Pi," *F&SF*, XVIII (May), 67–77.
  Adding a Dimension, 1964, pp. 38–49.

"The Bug-Eyed Vonster," *F&SF*, XVIII (June), 73–83.

Book reviews, *Hornbook*, XXXVI (June), 226–228.

"Beyond the Phyla," *Astounding*, LXV (July), 83–105.

F "The Covenant," Part two, *Fantastic*, IX (July), 6–46.
  [A "round robin" novel written with Poul Anderson, Robert Scheckley, Murray Leinster, and Robert Bloch.]
  Most Thrilling Science Fiction Ever Told, no. 2 (1966), 13–20.

"Beyond Pluto," *F&SF*, XVIII (July), 65–75.
  Fact and Fancy, 1962, pp. 109–122.

"Catskills in the Sky," *F&SF*, XIX (August), 89–99.
  Fact and Fancy, 1962, pp. 96–108.

Book reviews, *Hornbook*, XXXVI (August), 305–308.

"The Matter of Space," *Astounding*, LXVI (September),
83–98.

"Tools of the Trade," *F&SF*, XIX (September), 69–78.
Adding a Dimension, 1964, pp. 50–59.

F "Thiotimoline and the Space Age," *Analog*, LXVI (October),
155–162.
Opus 100, 1969, pp. 175–184.
Judith Merril, ed. *The 6th Annual of the Year's Best S F*. New
York: Simon & Schuster, 1961, pp. 175–183.

"Stepping-Stones to the Stars," *F&SF*, XIX (October),
82–91.
Fact and Fancy, 1962, pp. 123–136.

Book reviews, *Hornbook*, XXXVI (October), 415–417.

"The Hungry People," *Mademoiselle*, LI (October),
118–119, 147–148.
Is Anyone There? 1967, pp. 29–36.

"The Element of Perfection," *F&SF*, XIX (November),
79–89.
View from a Height, 1963, pp. 63–76.

"Now Hear This!" *F&SF*, XIX (December), 59–69.
View from a Height, 1963, pp. 109–122.

Book reviews, *Hornbook*, XXXVI (December), 521–524.

1961

The Bloodstream: *River of Life*. See *The Living River*, 1960.

F *Foundation Trilogy*. Garden City, N.Y.: Doubleday.
[Contents: *Foundation*, 1951; *Foundation and Empire*,
1952; *Second Foundation*, 1953.] London: Sidgwick &
Jackson, 1966, under the title *An Isaac Asimov Omnibus*.

The Realm of Algebra. Boston: Houghton Mifflin. Toronto: T. Allen, 1961. London: Gollancz, 1961. Greenwich, Conn.: Fawcett, 1967, 1970.

F *Triangle.* Garden City, N.Y.: Doubleday. [Contents: *The Currents of Space*, 1952; *Pebble in the Sky*, 1950; and *The Stars, Like Dust*, 1951.] London: Sidgwick & Jackson, 1969, under the title *An Isaac Asimov Second Omnibus.*

Words from the Myths. Boston: Houghton Mifflin. Toronto: T. Allen, 1961. London: Faber & Faber, 1963. Eau Claire, Wisc.: Hale, 1966. New York: New American Library (Signet), 1969.

Contributing editor for biochemistry to: *Stedman's Medical Dictionary*, 20th edition. Baltimore: Williams & Wilkins. 21st edition, 1966.

"Here It Comes; There It Goes!" *F&SF*, xx (January), 84–93.
Fact and Fancy, 1962, pp. 207–219.

"Order! Order!" *F&SF*, xx (February), 93–104.
View from a Height, 1963, pp. 135–150.

"Views on Science Books," *Hornbook*, xxxvii (February), 70–71.

F "Playboy and the Slime God," *Amazing*, xxxv (March), 30–43.
Nightfall, 1969, pp. 308-320, under the title "What Is This Thing Called Love?"

"The Imaginary That Isn't," *F&SF*, xx (March), 66–76.
Adding a Dimension, 1964, pp. 60–70.

"Imagination in Orbit," *The Writer*, LXXIV (March), 16–18, 36. [A rewrite of "Other Worlds to Conquer," May 1951.]
A. S. Burack, ed. *The Writer's Handbook*. Boston: The Writer, Inc. 1964, 1965, 1966, 1967, pp. 309–315.

"My Built-in Doubter," *F&SF*, XX (April), 75–85.
Sci Di, LII (July 1962), 36–43, under the title "The Value of Doubting."
Fact and Fancy, 1962, pp. 237–250.

"Views on Science Books," *Hornbook*, XXXVII (April), 175–176.

"Heaven on Earth," *F&SF*, XX (May), 85–94.
Fact and Fancy, 1962, pp. 153–166.

"We, the In-Betweens," *Mademoiselle*, LIII (May), 136–137, 84, 87–88.
Is Anyone There? 1967, pp. 191–196.

"Four Steps to Salvation," *F&SF*, XX (June), 93–103.

"Views on Science Books," *Hornbook*, XXXVII (June), 281–282.

"Recipe for a Planet," *F&SF*, XXI (July), 70–79.
Sci Di, L (September 1961), 33–38, under the title "What Is the Earth Made Of?"
View from a Height, 1963, pp. 197–210.

"The Evens Have It," *F&SF*, XXI (August), 102–112.
View from a Height, 1963, pp. 91–107.

"Views on Science Books," *Hornbook*, XXXVII (August), 358-359.

"Not as We Know It," *F&SF*, XXI (September), 82–92.
View from a Height, 1963, pp. 47–61.

"Measuring Rods in Space," *Space World*, I (September),
40–41, 56–58.
Is Anyone There? 1967, pp. 150–157.

"That's About the Size of It," *F&SF*, xxi (October), 70–79.
View from a Height, 1963, pp. 3–16.

F "The Machine That Won the War," *F&SF*, xxi (October),
51–55.
Nightfall, 1969, pp. 322-327.
Robert Mills, ed. *The Best from Fantasy and S F, 11th series*.
Garden City, N.Y.: Doubleday, 1962, pp. 76–81.

"Views on Science Books," *Hornbook*, xxxvii (October),
454–455.

"Dethronement," *F&SF*, xxi (November), 67–76.

"Fact Catches Up With Fiction," New York *Times Magazine*,
November 19, vi, pp. 34, 39, 42, 44.

"The Trojan Hearse," *F&SF*, xxi (December), 61–70.
View from a Height, 1963, pp. 211–224.

"Views on Science Books," *Hornbook*, xxxvii (December),
564–565.

"The Flaming Element," *Petroleum Today*, iii (Winter
1961–1962), 22–24.
Is Anyone There? 1967, pp. 93–101.

1962

Fact and Fancy. Garden City, N.Y.: Doubleday.

Life and Energy. Garden City, N.Y.: Doubleday. London:
Dobson, 1963. New York: Bantam, 1965. New York:
Avon, 1972.

Marvels of Science. See Only a Trillion, 1957.

The Search for the Elements. New York: Basic Books. New York: Fawcett, 1966, 1971.

Words in Genesis. Boston: Houghton Mifflin. Toronto: T. Allen, 1962.

Words on the Map. Boston: Houghton Mifflin. Eau Claire, Wisc.: Hale, 1965.
Excerpt, *Opus 100*, 1969, pp. 220–223.

F *The Hugo Winners.* Isaac Asimov, ed. Garden City, N.Y.: Doubleday. London: Dobson, 1962. New York: Avon, 1963.
The Hugo Winners, 2 vols. in 1. New York: Science Fiction Book Club, 1972.

Introduction to *Soviet Science Fiction.* Translated by Violet L. Dutt. New York: Collier, pp. 7–13.

Introduction to *More Soviet Science Fiction.* Translated by Rosa Prokof'va. New York: Collier, pp. 7–13.

"Isaac Asimov on Science," in *World Book Year Book.* Chicago: Field Enterprises, pp. 22–27.

"The Modern Demonology," *F&SF*, XXII (January), 73–83.
View From a Height, 1963, pp. 151–164.

"The Meaning of the New Physics," *Sci Di*, LI (January), 67–74.

"Superficially Speaking," *F&SF*, XXII (February), 78–88.
View From a Height, 1963, pp. 239–250.

"Views on Science Books," *Hornbook*, XXXVIII (February), 68–69.

F "My Son, The Physicist," *Scientific American*, CCVI (February), 110–111. [In an advertisement for Hoffman Electronics.]
Nightfall, 1969, 329–332.

"That's Life!" *F&SF*, XXII (March), 78–88.
View From a Height, 1963, pp. 31–46.

"The Weighting Game," *F&SF*, XXII (April), 103–112.
View From a Height, 1963, pp. 77–90.

"Views on Science Books," *Hornbook*, XXVIII (April), 194–195.

"Blood Will Tell," *Think*, XXVIII (April), 15–17.
Is Anyone There? 1967, pp. 37–43.

"By Jove!" *F&SF*, XXII (May), 55–64.
View From a Height, 1963, pp. 225–238.

"The Egg and Wee," *F&SF*, XXII (June), 75–85.
View From a Height, 1963, pp. 17–30.

"Views on Science Books," *Hornbook*, XXXVIII (June), 301–302.

"Hot Stuff," *F&SF*, XXIII (July), 99–108.
View From a Height, 1963, pp. 183–196.

"The Light Fantastic," *F&SF*, XXIII (August), 53–63.
Adding a Dimension, 1964, pp. 108–118.

"Views on Science Books," *Hornbook*, XXXVIII (August), 391–392.

"The Shape of Things," *F&SF*, XXIII (September), 89–99.
Adding a Dimension, 1964, pp. 168–179.

"Slow Burn," *F&SF*, XXIII (October), 52–62.
Adding a Dimension, 1964, pp. 120–131.

"Views on Science Books," *Hornbook*, XXXVIII (October),
500–501.

F "Starlight," *Scientific American*, CCVII (October), 76–77.
[In an advertisement for Hoffman Electronics.]
Fortune, LXVI (November) 170–171 [advertisement].
Asimov's Mysteries, 1968, 174–77.
John Carnell, ed. *New Writings in S F—4*. New York: Bantam,
1968.

"Pre-fixing It Up," *F&SF*, XXIII (November), 43–52.
Adding a Dimension, 1964, pp. 71–81.

"One, Ten, Buckle My Shoe," *F&SF*, XXIII (December),
57–68.
Adding a Dimension, 1964, pp. 14–26.

"Views on Science Books," *Hornbook*, XXXVIII (December),
616–617.

1963

The Genetic Code. New York: Orion. New York: New
American Library, 1963. New York: Ambassador, 1964.

The Human Body: Its Structure and Operation. Boston:
Houghton Mifflin. Toronto: T. Allen, 1963. New York:
New American Library, 1964. London: Nelson, 1965.

The Kite That Won the Revolution. Boston: Houghton
Mifflin. Toronto: T. Allen, 1963.

Marvels of Science. See Only a Trillion, 1958.

F *The 1,000 Year Plan. See Foundation*, 1951.

View From a Height. Garden City, N.Y.: Doubleday.
London: Dobson, 1964. New York: Lancer, 1969.

Words From the Exodus. Boston: Houghton Mifflin. Toronto: T. Allen, 1963.

F *Fifty Short Science Fiction Tales.* Isaac Asimov and Groff Conklin, eds. New York: Collier. Introduction by Isaac Asimov, pp. 11–15.

Articles contributed to *Encyclopedia International.* New York: Grolier, Inc. Alkali Metals, Alkaline-Earth Metals, Aluminum or Aluminium, Antimony, Argon, Arsenic, Atom, Atomic Energy, Atomic Power, Barium, Beryllium, Boron, Cadmium, Calcium, Carbon, Cesium, Chemical, Chlorine, Chromium, Cobalt, Copper, Element, Fluorine, Gallium, Germanium, Halogens, Hydrogen, Iodine, Iron, Lead, Lithium, Magnesium, Manganese, Mercury, Metal, Molybdenum, Nickel, Nitrogen, Oxygen, Periodic Table, Phosphorus, Platinum, Plutonium, Potassium, Radium, Radon, Silicon, Silver, Sodium, Strontium, Sulfur, Tantalum, Telurium, Thorium, Titanium, Transition Elements, Transuranium Elements, Uranium, Vanadium, Zinc, Zirconium.

Foreword to *The Unknown*, D. R. Benson, ed. New York: Pyramid, pp. 7–9.

"Isaac Asimov on Science," in *World Book Year Book.* Chicago: Field Enterprises, pp. 28–33.

"He's Not My Type," *F&SF*, xxiv (January), 37–46.
Adding a Dimension, 1964, pp. 156–166.

"Chemical You," *Mademoiselle*, lvi (January), 90–91, 118.
Is Anyone There? 1967, pp. 44–49.

"The Lost Generation," *F&SF*, xxiv (February), 72–82.
Adding a Dimension, 1964, pp. 144–155.

"Views on Science Books," *Hornbook*, XXXIX (February), 81–82.

"You, Too, Can Speak Gaelic," *F&SF*, XXIV (March), 72–81.
Adding a Dimension, 1964, pp. 132–142.

"The Rigid Vacuum," *F&SF*, XXIV (April), 52–62.
Adding a Dimension, 1964, pp. 84–95.

"Views on Science Books," *Hornbook*, XXXIX (April), 192–193.

"Just Mooning Around," *F&SF*, XXIV (May), 100–110.
Of Time and Space and Other Things, 1965, pp. 74–85.

"The Light That Failed," *F&SF*, XXIV (June), 84–94.
Adding a Dimension, 1964, pp. 96–107.

"Views on Science Books," *Hornbook*, XXXIX (June), 301–302.

"The Isaac Winners," *F&SF*, XXV (July), 95–104.
Adding a Dimension, 1964, pp. 192-204.

"T–Formation," *F&SF*, XXV (August), 46–55.
Adding a Dimension, 1964, pp. 2–13.

"Views on Science Books," *Hornbook*, XXXIX (August), 406–407.

"Who's Out There?" *F&SF*, XXV (September), 102–111.

"The Moon—First Stop in Space," *Science World*, Edition I, VII (September 27), 4–6, 23. First in a series.
Environments Out There, 1967, pp. 16–33.

"Twinkle, Twinkle Little Star," *F&SF*, XXV (October), 90–99.
Adding a Dimension, 1964, pp. 180–189.

"Views on Science Books," *Hornbook*, XXXIX (October), 518–519.

"The Hot Planets," *Science World*, Edition I, VII (October 25), 4–6.
Environments Out There, 1967, pp. 34–45, under the title "The Inside Planets."

"The Sword of Achilles," *Bulletin of Atomic Scientists*, XIX (November), 17–18.
Library Journal, LXXXIX (February 15, 1964), 914–917, under the title "SF: Clue to Creativity."
Is Anyone There? 1967, pp. 298–302.

"Welcome, Stranger," *F&SF*, XXV (November), 39–49.
Of Time and Space, 1965, pp. 168–179.

"Mars—the 'Maybe' Planet," *Science World*, Edition I, VII (November 22), 4–7.
Environments Out There, 1967, pp. 46–61, under the title "Mars after Mariner."

"Roll Call," *F&SF*, XXV (December), 96–106.
Of Time and Space, 1965, pp. 51–63.

"Views on Science Books," *Hornbook*, XXXIX (December), 613–614.

1964

Adding a Dimension. Garden City, N.Y.: Doubleday. Toronto: Dobson, 1966. New York: Lancer, 1970.

Asimov's Biographical Encyclopedia of Science and Technology. Garden City, N.Y.: Doubleday. New revised edition, Garden City, N.Y.: Doubleday, 1971.
Excerpt, *Opus 100*, 1969, pp. 128–136.

42

The Human Brain: Its Capacities and Functions. Boston:
Houghton Mifflin. Toronto: T. Allen, 1963. New York:
New American Library, 1965. London: Nelson, 1965.

*The Intelligent Man's Guide to the Biological Sciences.
See The Intelligent Man's Guide to Science*, 1960.

Planets for Man. With Stephen Dole. New York:
Random House.

Quick and Easy Math. Boston: Houghton Mifflin. Toronto:
T. Allen, 1964.
Condensation, *Popular Science*, CLXXXV (December 1964), 77–83.
Excerpt, *Opus 100*, 1969, pp. 95–103.

F *The Rest of the Robots*. Garden City, N.Y.: Doubleday.
Eight Stories from The Rest of the Robots. New York: Pyramid,
1966.

A Short History of Biology. Garden City, N.Y.: Doubleday,
Natural History Press [Published for the American
Museum of Natural History]. Garden City, N.Y.:
Doubleday, 1964. London: Nelson, 1965.

F "Author! Author!" in *The Unknown Five*, D. R. Benson, ed.
New York: Pyramid, pp. 15–42.
Early Asimov, 1972.

"Focus on Science," in *World Book Year Book*. Chicago:
Field Enterprises, pp. 30–35.

Foreword to *Introducing Science*, by Alan Isaacs. New York:
Basic Books, pp. 3–7.

"Round and Round and . . ." *F&SF*, XXVI (January), 104–113.
Of Time and Space, 1965, pp. 64–73.

"The Mysterious Asteroids—'Vermin of the Skies,' "
Science World, Edition I, VII (January 10), 4–6.
Environments Out There, 1967, pp. 62–73.

"The Slowly Moving Finger," *F&SF*, xxvi (February), 63–72.
Of Time and Space, 1965, pp. 193–202.

"Views on Science Books," *Hornbook*, xl (February), 79–80.

"The Giant Planets," *Science World*, Edition I, viii
(February 14), 6–9.
Environments Out There, 1967, pp. 74–85.

"Forget It!" *F&SF*, xxvi (March), 32–41.
Of Time and Space, 1965, pp. 122–133.

"Pluto and the Moons of the Giants," *Science World*,
Edition I, viii (March 13), 6–8.
Environments Out There, 1967, pp. 86–97.

"A Piece of the Action," *F&SF*, xxvi (April), 28–37.
Of Time and Space, 1965, pp. 157–167.

"Views on Science Books," *Hornbook*, xl (April), 197–198.

"The Search for Other Planets," *Science World*, Edition I,
viii (April 17), 6–8.
Environments Out There, 1967, pp. 98–109.

"Ghost Lines in the Sky," *F&SF*, xxvi (May), 93–102.
Of Time and Space, 1965, pp. 26–37.

"At Home in Space?" *Science World*, Edition I, viii
(May 15), 6–8.
Environments Out There, 1967, pp. 110–121.

"The Heavenly Zoo," *F&SF*, xxvi (June), 96–106.
Of Time and Space, 1965, pp. 38–50.

"Views on Science Books," *Hornbook*, xl (June), 303–304.

"Time-Travel: One-Way," *North American Review*, n. s.,
i (June), 20–23.
Is Anyone There? 1967, pp. 158–166.

44

"Nothing Counts," *F&SF*, xxvii (July), 80–90.
Of Time and Space, 1965, pp. 134–145.

"The Days of Our Years," *F&SF*, xxvii (August), 95–104.
Of Time and Space, 1965, pp. 2–13.

"Views on Science Books," *Hornbook*, xl (August),
394–395.

"Visit to the World's Fair of 2014," New York *Times Magazine*, August 16, vi, pp. 20, 32, 34, 36.
Is Anyone There? 1967, pp. 225–229.

"The Haste-Makers," *F&SF*, xxvii (September), 91–101.
Of Time and Space, 1965, pp. 180–192.

"First and Rearmost," *F&SF*, xxvii (October), 66–75.
Of Time and Space, 1965, pp. 86–97.

"Views on Science Books," *Hornbook*, xl (October),
513–514.

"The Black of Night," *F&SF*, xxvii (November), 72–81.
Of Time and Space, 1965, pp. 98–108.

"Hello, CTA–21, Is Anyone There?" New York *Times Magazine*, November 29, vi, pp. 52, 57, 59–60, 62, 64.
Is Anyone There? 1967, pp. 197–206, under the title "Is Anyone There?"
Whit Burnett, ed. *This Is My Best in the Third Quarter of the Century*. Garden City, N.Y.: Doubleday, 1970, pp. 871–880. ["America's 85 greatest living authors."]

"A Galaxy at a Time," *F&SF*, xxvii (December), 45–54.
Of Time and Space, 1965, pp. 109–120.

"Views on Science Books," *Hornbook*, xl (December),
660–661.

1965

An Easy Introduction to the Slide Rule. Boston: Houghton
Mifflin. New York: Fawcett, 1967, 1971.

The Greeks: A Great Adventure. Boston: Houghton Mifflin.
Excerpt, *Opus 100,* 1969, pp. 231–233.

*The Intelligent Man's Guide to the Physical Sciences. See
The Intelligent Man's Guide to Science,* 1960.

*The New Intelligent Man's Guide to Science. See The
Intelligent Man's Guide to Science,* 1960.

Of Time and Space and Other Things. Garden City, N.Y.:
Doubleday. New York: Lancer, 1968.

A Short History of Chemistry. Garden City, N.Y.: Doubleday.

"About Robert Silverberg," Introduction to *To Worlds
Beyond,* Robert Silverberg, ed. Philadelphia: Chilton,
pp. vii–ix.

"Focus on Science," in *World Book Year Book.* Chicago:
Field Enterprises, pp. 32–37.

"Life in 1990," *Diners Club Magazine.*
Sci Di, LVIII (August 1965), 63–70.
Is Anyone There? 1967, pp. 217–224, under the title "The World
of 1990."

"Begin at the Beginning," *F&SF,* XXVIII (January), 43–52.
Of Time and Space, 1965, pp. 14–25.

"Why I Wouldn't Have Done It This Way," *TV Guide,*
XIII (January 16), 26–28.
Is Anyone There? 1967, pp. 303–307, under the title "How Not
to Build a Robot."

"Harmony in Heaven," *F&SF*, XXVIII (February), 81–91.
From Earth to Heaven, 1966, pp. 173–184.

"Views on Science Books," *Hornbook*, XLI (February), 72–73.

"What Can We Expect of the Moon?" *American Legion Magazine*, LXXVIII (March), 8–11, 38–41.
Is Anyone There? 1967, pp. 239–250, under the title "The Moon and the Future."

"Oh, East Is East and West Is West—" *F&SF*, XXVIII (March), 80–89.
From Earth to Heaven, 1966, pp. 2–12.

"The Certainty of Uncertainty," *F&SF*, XXVIII (April), 104–114.
From Earth to Heaven, 1966, pp. 113–124.

F "Eyes Do More Than See," *F&SF*, XXVIII (April), 115–117.
Nightfall, 1969, pp. 334–336.
Edward L. Ferman, ed. *The Best From Fantasy and S F, 15th Series*. Garden City, N.Y.: Doubleday, 1966, pp. 129–133. Judith Merril, ed. *11th Annual of the Year's Best S F*. New York: Delacorte, 1966, pp. 214–217.

"Views on Science Books," *Hornbook*, XLI (April), 187–189.

"The New Enzymology," *Consultant*, V (May), 44–46.
Is Anyone There? 1967, pp. 50–55, under the title "The Survival of the Molecular Fittest."

"To Tell a Chemist," *F&SF*, XXVIII (May), 87–96.
From Earth to Heaven, 1966, pp. 101–112.

"Science in Search of a Subject," New York *Times Magazine*, May 23, VI, pp. 52–53, 55–56, 58.
Is Anyone There? 1967, pp. 183–190.

"Future? Tense!" *F&SF*, XXVIII (June), 100–109.
From Earth to Heaven, 1966, pp. 50–61.

"Views on Science Books," *Hornbook*, XLI (June), 302–303.

"Exclamation Point!" *F&SF*, XXIX (July), 104–113.
From Earth to Heaven, 1966, pp. 78–88.

"Behind the Teacher's Back," *F&SF*, XXIX (August), 71–80.
From Earth to Heaven, 1966, pp. 125–135.

"Views on Science Books," *Hornbook*, LXI (August),
413–414.

"What is a bubble chamber?" *Sci Di*, LVIII (August), 86–87.
First in a series entitled "Please Explain."

"Anatomy of a Man from Mars," *Esquire*, LXIV
(September), 113–117, 200.
Is Anyone There? 1967, pp. 207–211.

"Death in the Laboratory," *F&SF*, XXIX (September),
109–118.
From Earth to Heaven, 1966, pp. 89–100.

"Please explain [radio waves and other waves]," *Sci Di*,
LVIII (September), 97–98.

F "The Man Who Made the 21st Century," *Boys' Life*,
LV (October), 16–17, 66–67.

Isaac Asimov Replies [to a Russian criticism of American
science fiction], *F&SF*, XXIX (October), 64–65.

"The Land of Mu," *F&SF*, XXIX (October), 104–113.
From Earth to Heaven, 1966, pp. 136–147.

F "Founding Father," *Galaxy*, XXIV (October), 165–171.
Groff Conklin, ed. *13 Above the Night*. New York: Dell, 1965,
pp. 11–64. Henry Harrison, ed. *Authors' Choice*. New York:
Berkley, 1968, pp. 46–55.

"Views on Science Books," *Hornbook*, XLI (October),
515–516.

"Squ-u-u-ush!" *F&SF*, XXIX (November), 109–118.
From Earth to Heaven, 1966, pp. 185–196.

"All about 'bugs,' " *Sci Di*, LVII (November), 84–85.

"Water, Water Everywhere—" *F&SF*, XXIX (December), 78–87.
From Earth to Heaven, 1966, pp. 13–23.

"Views on Science Books," *Hornbook*, XLI (December), 646–647.

"Where do 'dead' satellites go?" *Sci Di*, LVIII (December), 87–88.

1966

F *Eight Stories from The Rest of the Robots. See The Rest of the Robots*, 1964.

F *Fantastic Voyage. See* "Fantastic Voyage," February 1966.

From Earth to Heaven. Garden City, N.Y.: Doubleday.

The Genetic Effects of Radiation. With Theodosius Dobzhansky. Washington: The U. S. Atomic Energy Commission.

F *An Isaac Asimov Omnibus. See Foundation Trilogy*, 1961.

The Neutrino, Ghost Particle of the Atom. Garden City, N.Y.: Doubleday. London: Dobson, 1966. New York: Dell, 1967.
Excerpt, *Opus 100*, 1969, pp. 140–146.

The Noble Gases. New York: Basic Books.
Excerpt, *Opus 100*, 1969, pp. 166–172.

The Roman Republic. Boston: Houghton Mifflin.
Excerpt, *Opus 100*, 1969, pp. 234–235.

F *The Thousand Year Plan. See Foundation*, 1951.

Understanding Physics. Vol. I, Motion, Sound and Heat;
Vol. II, Light, Magnetism, and Electricity; Vol. III,
The Electron, Proton, and Neutron. New York: Walker.
London: Allen & Unwin, 1967. Toronto: McLeod,
1967. New York: Signet, 1969.

The Universe: From Flat Earth to Quasar. New York:
Walker. Toronto: McLeod, 1966. London: Penguin, 1967.
New York: Avon Discus, 1968. Rev. ed. New York:
Walker, 1971.
Excerpt, *Opus 100*, 1969, pp. 41–54.

F *Tomorrow's Children.* Isaac Asimov, ed. Garden City,
N.Y.: Doubleday. Introduction by Isaac Asimov, pp. 9–12.

"Our Evolving Atmosphere," in *Science Year: The World
Book Science Annual.* Chicago: Field Enterprises,
pp. 198–209.
Is Anyone There? 1967, pp. 121–132.

"How Far Will We Go in Space?" in *World Book Year Book.*
Chicago: Field Enterprises, pp. 148–163.
Is Anyone There? 1967, pp. 251–260, under the title "The Solar
System and the Future."

"There's No Place Like Spome," in *Atmosphere in Space
Cabins and Closed Environments*, K. Kammermeyer, ed.
New York: Meredith, pp. 249–265.
Is Anyone There? 1967, pp. 261–280.

"The Proton-Reckoner," *F&SF*, xxx (January), 80–90.
From Earth to Heaven, 1966, pp. 197–208.

"How breeder reactors work," *Sci Di*, LIX (January), 84–85.

"Up and Down the Earth," *F&SF*, xxx (February), 91–101.
From Earth to Heaven, 1966, pp. 24–36.

"Views on Science Books," *Hornbook*, xlii (February),
78–79.

F "Fantastic Voyage," *Saturday Evening Post*, ccxxxix
(February 26), 40–44, 46–51, 53, 56–58, 60, 61; (March
12), 56–60, 62–68, 70, 73–77.
Fantastic Voyage [A novel based on the screenplay by Harry
Kleiner, from the original short story by Otto Klement and Jay
Lewis Bixby]. Boston: Houghton Mifflin, 1966. Toronto: T. Allen,
1966. London: Dobson, 1966. New York: Bantam, 1966, 1969.

"The properties of cosmic rays and neutrinos and how they
differ," *Sci Di*, lix (February), 91–92.

"Conceived in the Love-Bed of Science," *True*, xlvii
(February), 60–62, 85–86, 88–89.
Is Anyone There? 1967, pp. 71–90, under the title "Constructing
a Man."

"The Rocks of Damocles," *F&SF*, xxx (March), 94–103.
From Earth to Heaven, 1966, pp. 162–172.

"Please explain [fuel cells]," *Sci Di*, lix (March), 93–94.

"Can You Spot the Family Resemblance?" *TV Guide*,
xiv (March 3), 18–22.
Is Anyone There? 1967, pp. 308–312, under the title "The
Insidious Uncle Martin."

"The Nobelmen of Science," *F&SF*, xxx (April), 101–111.
From Earth to Heaven, 1966, pp. 62–76.

"Views on Science Books," *Hornbook*, xlii (April), 213–214.

"The Lovely Lost Landscapes of Luna," *P.S.*, i (April),
34–38.
Is Anyone There? 1967, pp. 313–320.

"Please explain [the planets' orbital plane]," *Sci Di*, LIX (April), 92–93.

"Time and Tide," *F&SF*, XXX (May), 106–116.
From Earth to Heaven, 1966, pp. 150–161.

"Relativity in 500 words," *Sci Di*, LIX (May), 82–83.

"The Isles of Earth," *F&SF*, XXX (June), 84–95.
From Earth to Heaven, 1966, pp. 37–49.

"Views on Science Books," *Hornbook*, XLII (June), 330–331.

"Please explain [replacement of body cells]," *Sci Di*, LIX (June), 83–84.

"UFO's, What I Think," *Sci Di*, LIX (June), 44–47.

"Balancing the Books," *F&SF*, XXXI (July), 83–93.
Science, Numbers, and I, 1968, pp. 3–15.

"That Odd Chemical Complex, the Human Mind,"
New York *Times Magazine*, July 3, VI, pp. 12–13, 16–18.
Is Anyone There? 1967, pp. 3–15, under the title "Matter Over Mind."

"Why does the moon show only one face?" *Sci Di*,
LX (July), 92–93.

"BB or Not BB, That Is the Question," *F&SF*, XXXI
(August), 103–113.
Science, Numbers and I, 1968, pp. 16–28.

"Views on Science Books," *Hornbook*, XLII (August),
454–455.

"How does an electron microscope work?" *Sci Di*, LX
(August), 88–89.

"I'm Looking Over a Four-Leaf Clover," *F&SF*, XXXI
(September), 89–99.
Science, Numbers and I, 1968, pp. 29–42.

52

"What is time?" *Sci Di*, LX (September), 93–94.

"Portrait of the Writer as a Boy," *F&SF*, XXXI (October), 46–55.
Science, Numbers and I, 1968, pp. 215–226.

F "The Key," *F&SF*, XXXI (October), 5–31.
Asimov's Mysteries, 1968, pp. 178–208.
Edward L. Ferman, ed. *The Best From Fantasy and S F, 16th Series*, Garden City, N.Y.: Doubleday, 1967, pp. 76–109.

"The Prime of Life" [poem], *F&SF*, XXXI (October), 56.

"Views on Science Books," *Hornbook*, XLII (October), 584–585.

"Pills to Help Us Remember?" New York *Times Magazine*, October 9, VI, pp. 38–39, 142, 144–151.
Is Anyone There? 1967, pp. 16–28, under the title "I Remember, I Remember."

"Old Man River," *F&SF*, XXXI (November), 105–114.
Science, Numbers and I, 1968, pp. 137–148.

"How was the earth's atmosphere formed?" *Sci Di*, LX (November), 91–92.

"What Are a Few Galaxies Among Friends," *TV Guide*, XIV (November 26), 6–9.

"The Symbol-Minded Chemist," *F&SF*, XXXI (December), 83–95.
Science, Numbers and I, 1968, pp. 82–94.

"Views on Science Books," *Hornbook*, XLII (December), 731–732.

"Is the speed of light ultimate?" *Sci Di*, LX (December), 87–88.

1967

The Egyptians. Boston: Houghton Mifflin.
Excerpt, *Opus 100*, 1969, pp. 236–238.

Environments Out There. London, New York: Abelard-Schuman. New York: Starline, 1971.
Material originally published in *Science World*, September 1963–May 1964.

Is Anyone There? Garden City, N.Y.: Doubleday. New York: Ace Books, 1968, 1970.

Mars. Chicago: Follett.

The Moon. Chicago: Follett.

The Roman Empire. Boston: Houghton Mifflin.

F *Through a Glass, Clearly*. London: New English Library.

To the Ends of the Universe. New York: Walker. Toronto: Ryerson, 1967.

"Acids and Bases," in *Merit Students Encyclopedia*. New York: Crowell-Collier Educational Corp.

"Colloid," in *Merit Students Encyclopedia*. New York: Crowell-Collier Educational Corp.

"Harlan and I," Introduction No. 2 in *Dangerous Visions*, Harlan Ellison, ed. Garden City, N.Y.: Doubleday, pp. xiii-xv.

"Let There Be a New Light," in *Is Anyone There?* 1967, pp. 102–114.

"Man and the Sun," in *Is Anyone There?* 1967, pp. 136–143.

"On Flying Saucers," in *Is Anyone There?* 1967, pp. 212–213.

"The Second Revolution," Introduction No. 1 in *Dangerous Visions*, Harlan Ellison, ed. Garden City, N.Y.: Doubleday, pp. vii–xii.

"There's Nothing Like a Good Foundation," *SFWA Bulletin*, III (January), 12–14.
Excerpt, *Opus 100*, 1969, pp. 240–242.

F "The Segregationist," *Abbottempo*, Book 4 (n. d.), 34–36.
F&SF, XXXV (October 1968), 80–84.
Nightfall, 1969, pp. 337–343.
Best S F: 1968, ed. by Harry Harrison & Brian Aldiss. New York: Putnam, 1969, pp. 82–88.

"The Price of Life," *Cavalier*, (Jan.)
Is Anyone There? 1967, pp. 234–238.

"Right Beneath Your Feet," *F&SF*, XXXII (January), 107–116.

"Where do sunken ships go?" *Sci Di*, LXI (January), 87–88.

"Moon Exploration: Advent of the New Engineering," *Technology Week*, XX (January 23), 46–48.

"Impossible, That's All!" *F&SF*, XXXII (February), 113–123.
Science, Numbers and I, 1968, pp. 43–56.

"Views on Science Books," *Hornbook*, XLIII (February), 91-92.

"Can you please give an explanation of the Unified Field Theory?" *Sci Di*, LXI (February), 86.

"Crowded!" *F&SF*, XXXII (March), 76–85.
Science, Numbers and I, 1968, pp. 149–160.

"Over the Edge of the Universe," *Harper's*, CCXXXIV (March), 97–98, 100, 103, 104, 106.
Is Anyone There? 1967, pp. 167–179, under the title "The Birth and Death of the Universe."

F "The Billiard Ball," *If*, XVII (March), 6–37.
   Asimov's Mysteries, 1968, pp. 209–228.
   Donald Wollheim and Terry Carr, eds. *World's Best Science
   Fiction, 4th Series*. New York: Ace Books, 1968, pp. 94–112.

"Where do stars come from?" *Sci Di*, LXI (March), 80–81.

"A Matter of Scale," *F&SF*, XXXII (April), 101–110.
   Science, Numbers and I, 1968, pp. 57–69.

"Views on Science Books," *Hornbook*, XLIII (April),
   224–225.

"Future Fun," *Lithopinion 6*, II (Second Quarter), 20–25.
   Infinity One, Robert Hoskins, ed. New York: Lancer, 1970,
   pp. 9–18 [introduction].

"What is parity?" *Sci Di*, LXI (April), 83–84. [With this
   issue, the title of the series was changed to "Isaac
   Asimov Explains."]

"Mr. Spock Is Dreamy," *TV Guide*, XV (April), 9–11.

"The Times of Our Lives," *F&SF*, XXXII (May), 105–115.
   Science, Numbers and I, 1968, pp. 173–185.

"After Apollo, a Colony on the Moon," New York *Times
   Magazine*, May 28, VI, pp. 30–32, 35, 37, 38, 40.
   Sci Di, LXII (September 1967), 44–48, 53–56.

"Backfire from speeding light," *Sci Di*, LXI (May), 85–86.

"Non-Time Travel," *F&SF*, XXXII (June), 82–91.
   Science, Numbers and I, 1968, pp. 186–198.

"Views on Science Books," *Hornbook*, XLIII (June),
   365–366.

"Is cosmic ray bombardment dangerous?" *Sci Di*,
   LXI (June), 87–88.

"Twelve Point Three Six Nine," *F&SF*, XXXIII (July), 102–111.

Science, Numbers and I, 1968, pp. 199–211. *Opus 100*, 1969, pp. 258–271.

"How vitamins work," *Sci Di*, LXII (July), 88–89.

"Kaleidoscope in the Sky," *F&SF*, XXXIII (August), 115–124. *Science, Numbers and I*, 1968, pp. 70–81.

"SF as a Stepping Stone" [guest editorial], *Galaxy*, XXV (August), 4, 6.

"Views on Science Books," *Hornbook*, XLIII (August), 493–494.

"Why we don't really know," *Sci Di*, LXII (August), 85–86.

"The Great Borning," *F&SF*, XXXIII (September), 106–116. *Science, Numbers and I*, 1968, pp. 95–107.

"About simultaneous discovery," *Sci Di*, LXII (September), 88–89.

"Music to My Ears," *F&SF*, XXXIII (October), 93–112. *Science, Numbers and I*, 1968, pp. 123–136.

"Views on Science Books," *Hornbook*, XLIII (October), 610–611. Last in the series.

"How did life begin?" *Sci Di*, LXII (October), 82–83.

"Knock Plastic!" *F&SF*, XXXIII (November), 101–110. *Science, Numbers and I*, 1968, pp. 108–120.

Book review of *The Way Things Work*, (New York, 1968), New York *Times*, November 19, VII, p. 3.

"What is meant by curved space?" *Sci Di*, LXII (November), 81–82.

"The First Metal," *F&SF*, XXXIII (December), 96–106.
The Solar System and Back, 1970, pp. 151–163.

"The Humanness of Man," *NEA Journal*, LVI (December),
6–8, 80–81.

"Nuclear Age Celebrates Silver Anniversary," *Sci Di*,
LXII (December), 44–48.

"The thinking machine," *Sci Di*, LXII (December), 73–74.

1968

Asimov's Guide to the Bible. Vol. I: The Old Testament.
Garden City, N.Y.: Doubleday.
Excerpt, *Opus 100*, 1969, pp. 255–258.

F *Asimov's Mysteries*. Garden City, N.Y.: Doubleday.
London: Rapp & Whiting, 1968. New York: Dell, 1969.

The Dark Ages. Boston: Houghton Mifflin.

Galaxies. Chicago: Follett.
Excerpt, *Opus 100*, 1969, pp. 54–55.

The Near East: *10,000 Years of History*. Boston:
Houghton Mifflin.
Excerpt, *Opus 100*, 1969, pp. 238–239.

Photosynthesis. New York: Basic Books.
Excerpt, *Opus 100*, 1969, pp. 201–207.

Science, Numbers and I. Garden City, N.Y.: Doubleday.
New York: Ace Books, 1969.

The Stars. Chicago: Follett.

F *A Whiff of Death. See The Death Dealers*, 1958.

Words from History. Boston: Houghton Mifflin.
Excerpt, *Opus 100*, 1969, pp. 223–226.

58

Articles contributed to *Encyclopedia Americana, International Edition.* New York: Americana Corp. Louis Agassiz, Antibodies and Antigens, ATP, Robert Brown, Anders Celsius, and Wetting Agents.

Introduction to *The Time Machine and The War of the Worlds*, by H. G. Wells. New York: Fawcett, pp. 9–22.

"On Prediction," introduction to *Future Tense*, Richard Curtis, ed. New York: Dell, pp. 7–10.
Opus 100, 1969, pp. 281–285.

"The Seventh Metal," *F&SF*, xxxiv (January), 101–110.
Solar System, 1970, pp. 164–176.

"Science fictionally speaking," *Sci Di*, lxii (January), 85–86.
Opus 100, 1969, pp. 276–278.

"The Predicted Metal," *F&SF*, xxxiv (February), 109–118.
Solar System, 1970, pp. 177–188.

"The death of the sun," *Sci Di*, lxiii (February), 89–90.

"The Seventh Planet," *F&SF*, xxxiv (March), 113–123.
Solar System, 1970, pp. 5–18.

"The fourth dimension," *Sci Di*, lxiii (March), 80–81.

"The Dance of the Sun," *F&SF*, xxiv (April), 80–91.
Solar System, 1970, pp. 19–32.

"Why is Pluto different?" *Sci Di*, lxiii (April), 80–81.

F "Exile to Hell," *Analog*, lxxxi (May), 50–53.

"Backward, Turn Backward—" *F&SF*, xxxiv (May), 92–103.
Solar System, 1970, pp. 33–46.

"Why ice floats," *Sci Di*, lxiii (May), 85–86.

"Children and Saturday Morning Cartoons," *TV Guide*, xvi (May 4), 6–10.

"Counting Chromosomes," *F&SF*, xxxiv (June), 93–102.
Solar System, 1970, pp. 218–231.

"The Scientific method," *Sci Di*, lxiv (June), 86–87.

Book review of *The Double Helix*, by James Watson (New York, 1968), *F&SF*, xxxv (July), 53–54.

F "Key Item," *F&SF*, xxxv (July), 76–79.

"Little Lost Satellite," *F&SF*, xxxv (July), 106–116.
Solar System, 1970, pp. 47–60.

"Birth of the oceans," *Sci Di*, lxiv (July), 71–72.

"The Terrible Lizards," *F&SF*, xxxv (August), 91–103.
Solar System, 1970, pp. 191–204.

"The greatest scientist ever," *Sci Di*, lxiv (August), 86–87.
[Sir Isaac Newton]

"Hitch Your Wagon to a Rock," *TV Guide*, xvi (August 31), 3–5.

F "The Proper Study," *Boys' Life*, lviii (September), 32, 69.

"The Dying Lizards," *F&SF*, xxxv (September), 108–118.
Solar System, 1970, pp. 205–217.

" 'Irresistible' vs. 'Immovable,' " *Sci Di*, lxiv (September), 89–90.
Opus 100, 1969, pp. 279–281.

"Little Found Satellite," *F&SF*, xxxv (October), 97–108.
Solar System, 1970, pp. 63–76.

"Subatomic bullets," *Sci Di*, lxiv (October), 82–83.

"The Perfect Machine," *Science Journal*, (October)
Excerpt, *Opus 100*, 1969, p. 60.

Letter to the editor, *If*, xviii (November), 160–161.

"The Planetary Eccentric," *F&SF*, xxxv (November),
91–102.
Solar System, 1970, pp. 104–118.

Book review of *In the Wake of the Sea Serpents*, by Bernard
Heuvelmans (New York, 1968), New York *Times*,
November 10, vii, pp. 46, 48.

"Faster than light," *Sci Di*, lxiv (November), 86–87.

"View from Amalthea," *F&SF*, xxxv (December), 88–99.
Solar System, 1970, pp. 77–90.
Excerpt, *Opus 100*, 1969, pp. 18–27.

F "The Holmes-Ginsbook Device," *If*, xviii (December), 5–14.
Opus 100, 1969, pp. 299–311.

"Sunspots—hot or cold?" *Sci Di*, lxiv, (December), 82–83.

1969

ABC's of Space. New York: Walker

Asimov's Guide to the Bible. Vol. II: The New Testament.
Garden City, N.Y.: Doubleday.

Great Ideas of Science. Boston: Houghton Mifflin.

F *An Isaac Asimov Second Omnibus. See Triangle*, 1961.

F *Nightfall, and Other Stories*. Garden City, N.Y.: Doubleday.
Greenwich, Conn.: Fawcett Crest, 1970.

Opus 100. Boston: Houghton Mifflin. New York: Dell, 1970.

The Shaping of England. Boston: Houghton Mifflin.

Twentieth Century Discovery. Garden City, N.Y.:
Doubleday. New York: Ace Books, 1969, 1970.

"In Memoriam: Groff Cronklin," in *Nebula Award Stories
Four*, Poul Anderson, ed. Garden City, N.Y.:
Doubleday, 1969, p. 221.

"That Plaque on the Moon," in *Men on the Moon*,
Donald Wollheim, ed. New York: Ace Books, p. 148.

"Life," in *Collier's Encyclopedia*. New York: Crowell-Collier
Educational Corporation.

"Dance of the Satellites," *F&SF*, xxxvi (January), 105–115.
Solar System, 1970, pp. 91–103.

"An Uncompromising View," book review of *Mechanical
Man, the Physical Basis of Intelligent Life*, by Dean E.
Wooldridge (New York: 1968), *The Physics Teacher*,
vii (January), 55–56.
Opus 100, 1969, pp. 287–289.

"Biological clocks," *Sci Di*, lxv (January), 78–79.

"Uncertain, Coy and Hard to Please," *F&SF*, xxxvi
(February), 104–115.
Solar System, 1970, pp. 232–246.

"The truth in Gödel's proof," *Sci Di*, lxv (February), 86, 88.

"Yipes, Cripes and Other Scientific Expressions,"
TV Guide, xvii (February 22), 6–8.

"Just Right," *F&SF*, xxxvi (March), 89–98.
Solar System, 1970, pp. 123–135.

"Imaginary numbers," *Sci Di*, lxv (March), 83–84.

"Husbands, Beware," *TV Guide*, xvii (March 22), 7–10.

"The Incredible Shrinking People," *F&SF*, XXXVI
(April), 107–117.
Solar System, 1970, pp. 136–148.

"And It Will Serve Us Right," *Psychology Today*, II
(April), 38–41, 64.

"Ordinary vs. binary numbers," *Sci Di*, LXV (April), 83–84.

"The Power of Progression," *F&SF*, XXXVI (May), 98–108.
The Stars in Their Courses, 1971, pp. 178–188.

"A Science Seance," with L. Sprague de Camp and Hal
Clement, *Science & Technology*, (May), 42–51.

"Can anti-gravity really exist?" *Sci Di*, LXV (May), 86–87.

"Excitement on the Moon," *Boys' Life*, LIX (June),
22–23, 50, 51, 59.

"The Fateful Lightning," *F&SF*, XXXVI (June), 108–118.
Stars, 1971, pp. 155–165.

"What is theoretical physics?" *Sci Di*, LXV (June), 85–86.

"Two at a Time," *F&SF*, XXXVII (July), 102–111.
Stars, 1971, pp. 49–59.

"Speed Limit 186,300 MPS," *Holiday*, XLVI (July),
40, 41, 72–74.

"The Moon Could Answer the Riddle of Life," New York
Times Magazine, July 13, VI, pp. 12–15, 17, 18, 20, 23, 26.
Condensation, *Sci Di*, LXVI (October 1969), 8–17, under the title
"Why We Must Explore the Moon."

"Spacecraft, Like Squid, Maneuver by 'Squirts,' " New
York *Times*, July 17, Special Supplement, p. 43.

"Refraction vs. diffraction," *Sci Di*, LXVI (July), 74–75.

"On Throwing a Ball," *F&SF*, XXXVII (August), 98–107.
Stars, 1971, pp. 60–70.

"Man Getting Better at Deciphering Cosmic Messages,"
New York *Times*, August 3, Special Supplement, "The
Moon: A New Frontier," pp. 18–19.

"Traveling faster than light," *Sci Di*, LXVI (August), 74–75.

"The Man Who Massed the Earth," *F&SF*, XXXVII
(September), 100–110.
Stars, 1971, pp. 71–81.

"Do antiparticles produce antienergy?" *Sci Di*, LXVI
(September), 80–81.

F "Feminine Intuition," *F&SF*, XXXVII (October), 4–23.
[A new Susan Calvin story.]
Edward L. Ferman & Robert P. Mills, eds. *Twenty Years of the
Magazine of Fantasy and Science Fiction*. New York: Putnam,
1970, pp. 80–101.

"Worlds in Confusion," *F&SF*, XXXVII (October), 52–61.
Stars, 1971, pp. 36–46.

"A neutrino is a neutrino," *Sci Di*, LXVI (October), 87–88.

"The Sin of the Scientist," *F&SF*, XXXVII (November), 81–90.
Stars, 1971, pp. 166–177.

"Asimov Replies" [to a review of *Opus 100*], *Luna*,
no. 6 (November), 9.

"A sizable universe," *Sci Di*, LXVI (November), 88–89.

"NASA Goofed!" *TV Guide*, XVII (November 8), 6–9.

"The Luxon Wall," *F&SF*, XXXVII (December), 96–105.
Stars, 1971, pp. 82–92.

"We Came in Peace for All Mankind," *Redbook*, CXXXIV (December), 151.

"How fast is infinite speed?" *Sci Di*, LXVI (December), 82–83.

1970

The ABC's of the Ocean. New York: Walker.

Asimov's Guide to Shakespeare, vols. 1–2. Garden City, N.Y.: Doubleday.

Constantinople. Boston: Houghton Mifflin.

Light. New York: Follett.

To the Solar System and Back. Garden City, N.Y.: Doubleday.

Introduction to *First Flights to the Moon*, Hal Clement, ed. Garden City, N. Y.: Doubleday, pp. xvii–xx.

Introduction to *Rings Around Tomorrow* by Hugh Downs. Garden City, N.Y.: Doubleday, pp. 9–10.

"Moon Exploration," in *Merit Students Encyclopedia*, New York: Crowell-Collier Educational Corporation.

"F & SF and I," foreword to *Twenty Years of the Magazine of Fantasy and Science Fiction*, Edward L. Ferman and Robert P. Mills, eds. New York: Putnam, pp. 1–5.

"The Lunar Honor-roll," *F&SF*, XXXVIII (January), 104–113.
Stars, 1971, pp. 3–13.

"All for an ounce of matter," *Sci Di*, LXVII (January), 67–68.

"Why do crystals form and why always in a certain shape?" *Sci Di*, LXVII (January), 68–69.

"Outer Space, Wet Space," *Seventeen*, XXIX (January), 82–83.

"The Multiplying Elements," *F&SF*, XXXVIII (February), 106–116.
Stars, 1971, pp. 117–127.

"Bettering the Good Book" [A review of *The New English Bible*], *Saturday Review*, LIII (February 28), 46–49.

"What is this thing called 'polywater'?" *Sci Di*, LXVII (February), 80–81.

"Bridging the Gaps," *F&SF*, XXXVIII (March), 100–112.
Stars, 1971, pp. 128–140.

"The Sun Vanishes," *Look*, XXXIV (March 10), 68–72.

"Polarizing light," *Sci Di*, LXVII (March), 72–73.

"The Nobel Prize That Wasn't," *F&SF*, XXXVIII (April), 105–114.

F "Waterclap," *If*, XX (April), 4–34.

"To Go Forward or Not After Near Disaster?" New York *Times*, April 19, IV, 1–2.

Letter to the editor [replying to criticism of book review], *Saturday Review*, LIII (April 11), 38.

"The hottest stars," *Sci Di*, LXVII (April), 80–81.

"Neglected Books" [one of about sixty replies to a request to name the most neglected books of the last 25 years], *American Scholar*, XXXIX (Spring), 318.

"A Problem of Numbers," *Ellery Queen's Mystery Magazine*, LV (May), 88–92.
Ellery Queen, ed. *Ellery Queen's Headliners: 20 Stories from Ellery Queen's Mystery Magazine*, 26th annual. New York: World, 1971, pp. 181–185.

"Playing the Game," *F&SF*, XXXVII (May), 88–98.
Stars, 1971, pp. 93–103.

"The Unseen World," *Harper's*, CCXL (May), 12–13
[advertisement for TV program with same title, for which
Asimov also wrote the script].

"Pulsars—what are they?" *Sci Di*, LXVII (May), 88–89.

"Science Fiction, an Aid to Science, Foresees the Future,"
Smithsonian, I (May), 40–46.

"How I Lost my Purity and Began Writing for Television,"
TV Guide, XVIII (May 2), 19–23.

"The Distance of Far," *F&SF*, XXXVIII (June), 105–114.
Stars, 1971, pp. 104–114.

"Where did all the dinosaurs go?" *Sci Di*, LXVII (June),
79–80.

"My Planet 'tis of Thee—" *F&SF*, XXXIX (July), 109–118.
Stars, 1971, pp. 189–199.

"The Case Against Man," *Long Island Press*, July 5,
1970, pp. 17–

"Why not green hot?" *Sci Di*, LXVIII (July), 78–79.

"The Stars in Their Courses," *F&SF*, XXXIX (August),
108–117.
Stars, 1971, pp. 3–13.

"Neutron stars—astronomical heavyweights," *Sci Di*,
LXVIII (August), 89–90.

"In the Game of Energy and Thermodynamics, You Can't
Even Break Even," *Smithsonian*, I (August), 4–11.

"The Lopsided Sun," *F&SF*, XXXIX (September), 99–108.
Stars, 1971, pp. 14–24.

"Controlled fusion," *Sci Di*, LXVIII (September), 89–90.

"Stop!" *F&SF*, XXXIX (October), 80–89.

"The Fourth Revolution," *Saturday Review*, LIII (October 24), 17–20.

"How can hydrogen be a metal?" *Sci Di*, LXVIII (October), 87–88.

"—But How?" *F&SF*, XXXIX (November), 96–105.

"What is a quark?" *Sci Di*, LXVIII (November), 89–90.

"The Thalassogens," *F&SF*, XXXIX (December), 94–104.

"What is the purpose of aging?" *Sci Di*, LXVIII (December), 76–77.

1971

ABC's of the Earth. New York: Walker.

F *Best New Thing*. New York: World.

The Isaac Asimov Treasury of Humor. Boston: Houghton Mifflin.

The Land of Canaan. Boston: Houghton Mifflin.

The Sensuous Dirty Old Man. [pseud. Dr. A.] New York: Walker.

The Space Dictionary. New York: Starline.

The Stars in Their Courses. Garden City, N.Y.: Doubleday.

What Makes the Sun Shine. Boston: Little, Brown.

F *The Hugo Winners*, vol. II. Isaac Asimov, ed. Garden City, N.Y.: Doubleday.

The Hugo Winners, 2 vols. in 1. New York: Science Fiction Book Club, 1972.

F *Where Do We Go From Here?* Isaac Asimov, ed. Garden City, N.Y.: Doubleday.

Foreword to *Four Futures*, by R. A. Lafferty and others. New York: Hawthorne

Introduction to *Ignition: An Informal History of Liquid Rocket Propellants.* John D. Clark. New Brunswick, N.J.: Rutgers University Press.

"Reaching for the Moon: An Introduction," in *The Man in the Moone: and Other Lunar Fantasies.* Faith Z. Pizor and Allen T. Camp, compilers. New York: Praeger, pp. xi–xx.

"Hot Water," *F&SF*, xl (January), 107–117.

"Bookworm," *Saturday Review*, liv (January 23), 70.

"What Is the 'Coriolis Effect'?" *Sci Di*, lxix (January), 82–83.

"Cold Water," *F&SF*, xl (February), 109–118.

"The low temperature of space," *Sci Di*, lxix (February), 76–77.

Letter, *The WSFA Journal*, No. 75 (February–March), 41–42.

"Euclid's Fifth," *F&SF*, xl (March), 111–121.

"No Space for Women?" *Ladies Home Journal*, lxxxviii (March), 115, 201, 202, 204.

"What are the 'mascons' on the moon?" *Sci Di*, lxix (March), 72–73.

"The Plane Truth," *F&SF*, xl (April), 101–110.

"What is beyond the Universe?" *Sci Di*, LXIX (April), 69–70.

"The Greeks' Four Universal Elements—and Then Some," *Smithsonian*, II (April), 33–39.

"Pompey and Circumstance," *F&SF*, XL (May), 94–104.

"Mystery of the one-way heat trap," *Sci Di*, LXIX (May), 82–83.

"The Eureka Phenomenon," *F&SF*, XL (June), 107–116.

"Electrons and the speed of light," *Sci Di*, LXIX (June), 88–89.

"TV's Race With Doom," *TV Guide*, XIX (June 5), 5–8.

"Bill and I," *F&SF*, XLI (July), 101–110.

"Can light exert a force on matter?" *Sci Di*, LXX (July), 44–45.

"Air, Thin Air, the Formless Element of the Greeks," *Smithsonian*, II (July), 24–31.

"Prime Quality," *F&SF*, XLI (August), 115–124.

"The Father of Science Fiction," *Luna*, No. 27, supplement (August).

"Shooting stars—fireworks in the sky," *Sci Di*, LXX (August), 82–83.

"Holes in the Head," *F&SF*, XLI (September), 85–94.

"Storms from the sun," *Sci Di*, LXX (September), 87–88.

"How the Greeks' Element, Water, Turned Into H_2O," *Smithsonian*, II (September), 26–31.

"Odds and Evens," *F&SF*, XLI (October), 91–99.

"How many quarks in a proton?" *Sci Di*, LXX (October), 82–83.

"The Left Hand of the Electron," *F&SF*, XLI (November), 101–110.

"How will the earth end?" *Sci Di*, LXX (November), 75–76.

"In Dancing Flames a Greek Saw the Basis of the Universe," *Smithsonian*, II (November), 52–57.

"Seeing Double," *F&SF*, XLI (December), 108–117.

"When Aristotle Fails, Try Science Fiction," *Intellectual Digest*, II (December), 75–77.

"Hidden Rhythms That Make Nature's Clock Tick," *National Wildlife*, X (December 1971–Jan. 1972), 34–40.

"How Many Inches in a Mile?" *Saturday Evening Post*, CCXLIII (Winter), 96–98, 128.

"Time measurement baffles scientist," *Sci Di*, LXX (December), 74–75.

1972

ABC's of Ecology. New York: Walker.

Asimov's Guide to Science, see The Intelligent Man's Guide to Science, 1960.

The Early Asimov. Garden City, N.Y.: Doubleday.

F *The Gods Themselves. See* "The Gods Themselves," March 1972.

The Left Hand of the Electron. Garden City, N.Y.: Doubleday.

More Words of Science. Boston: Houghton Mifflin.

"*In Re* Sprague," Introduction to *The Continent Makers*, L. Sprague de Camp. New York: New American Library/Signet, pp. ix-xiii.

"The Romance of Mars," Introduction to *Mars, We Love You*, Jane Hipolito and Willis E. McNelly, eds. Garden City, N.Y.: Doubleday, pp. xv–xx.

"The 3-D Molecule," *F&SF*, XLII (January), 95–103.

"What would happen if the ice-caps melted?" *Sci Di*, LXXI (January), 79–80.

"World's Most Deadly Poison . . . the Botulin Spore," *Sci Di*, LXXI (January), 8–11.

"The Asymmetry of Life," *F&SF*, XLII (February), 106-116.

"Why does the speed of sound vary?" *Sci Di*, LXXI (February), 92–93.

"Lost in Non-Translation," *F&SF*, XLII (March), 124–134.

F "The Gods Themselves," Part One, *Galaxy*, XXXII (March–April), 6–55. Part Two, *If*, XXI (March-April), 6–71. Part Three, *Galaxy*, XXXII (May–June), 4–85. *The Gods Themselves*. Garden City, N.Y.: Doubleday, 1972.

"How fast is gravity?" *Sci Di*, LXXI (March), 74–75.

"Moon Over Babylon," *F&SF*, XLII (April), 112–122.

"Are oceans getting too salty?" *Sci Di*, LXXI (April), 73–74.

F "The Computer That Went on Strike," *Saturday Evening Post*, CCXLIV (Spring), 74–75.

F "Mirror Image," *Analog*, LXXXIX (May), 149–162.

"Academe and I," *F&SF*, XLII (May), 133–143.

"When light is trapped," *Sci Di*, LXXI (May), 66–67.

"The Manhattan Project," *TV Guide*, XX (May 6, 12–15.

II. Selected Criticism and Works about Asimov

Aldiss, Brian. *The Shape of Further Things*. Garden City, N.Y.: Doubleday, 1971.

Only one chapter in this work deals explicitly with science fiction. Aldiss doesn't deal with Asimov at any length (pp. 33, 45–46, 106); he mentions him as one of the major science fiction writers developed by Campbell; says he believes Asimov's robots could never pass for human beings because they would lack that essential human feeling for other people's emotions and thoughts (p. 33).

Atheling, William, Jr. [James Blish] *The Issue at Hand*. Chicago: Advent, 1964.

Critical essays on science fiction, written for fanzines between 1952 and 1963. Atheling says Asimov's style is suited to "reflective" stories, such as the robot series, or stories covering a broad span of "history," such as the Foundation novels, but inappropriate for action stories like *The Stars, Like Dust*, and *The Currents of Space*.

Bear, Greg. "The TV and Dr. A." *Luna*, No. 1 (June 1969), 5.

A "review" of Isaac Asimov's appearance on the Mike Douglas show (April 28, 1969). Refers to Asimov as "the acknowledged Dean of Science Fiction."

Benjamin, Judy-Lynn. "A Thinking Woman's Philtre." *Luna*, No. 5 (October 1969), 14–17.

Miss Benjamin, of *Galaxy*, describes what a lady editor has to go through to get an sf story out of Asimov now that he is writing almost all non-fiction.

De Camp, L. Sprague. "You Can't Beat Brains," *F&SF*, xxxi
(October 1966), 32–35.

A friendly, chatty "appreciation" of Asimov as one of the boys—
but probably the smartest one.

Glicksohn, Susan. "A City of Which the Stars are Suburbs,"
in *SF: The Other Side of Realism*, Thomas D. Clareson, ed.
Bowling Green, Ohio: Bowling Green University Press,
1971, pp. 334–347.

An analysis of Stapledon's *Last and First Men* and *Asimov's
Foundation Trilogy*. Both, Glicksohn says, depict man's gradual
conquest of physical space; both also show human history as a
recurrent cycle within which man's nature and his myths do not
really change.

Goble, Neil. *Asimov Analyzed*. Baltimore: Mirage Press.
Scheduled for publication early in 1972.

Not available in time for annotation. Will deal with Asimov as
a science writer.

Harrison, Harry. Foreword to "Nightfall," in *The Mirror of
Infinity*. Robert Silverberg, ed. New York: Harper & Row,
1970, pp. 51–54.

Harrison sees "Nightfall" as typical, in both its strengths and its
weaknesses, of the best science fiction of its time. It is a story of
ideas told in "quiet and efficient" prose, with a fast pace, well
sustained until the satisfying climax. "Nightfall's" world was
carefully worked out in Asimov's mind, and suggested to the
reader through well-chosen, consistent details, rather than fully
described. Harrison calls Asimov a major science fiction writer,
and "Nightfall" a "landmark in the development of the entire
genre."

Huxley, N. P. "Coming of the Humanoids: Android Fiction,"
Commonweal, xci (December 5, 1969), 297–300.

Rephrases the Three Laws of Robotics—to no improvement—and
cites their influence on the work of other science fiction authors.

"An Isaac Asimov Bibliography," *F&SF*, XXXI (October 1966), 36–45.

Lists first appearances of fiction and non-fiction, books and periodicals, from 1939 to 1966. Does not include anthologies, foreign publications, or minor items such as encyclopedia articles, introductions, and letters to editors.

Klein, Jay Kay. "ESFA Open Meeting–1970," *The WSFA Journal*, No. 73 (September–November 1970), 11–22.

A typical fanzine report on Asimov's role at an SF convention— fun and games all around. This is the publication of the Washington, D.C., Science Fiction Association.

Knight, D. F. "Asimov and Empire," in *In Search of Wonder*. Chicago: Advent, 1967, pp. 90–94.

Knight admires Asimov's work greatly, except for the Galactic Empire stories, which he finds dull and unconvincing. "Nightfall" is "matchless of its kind;" *Caves of Steel* is "brilliant, thorough, and . . . an original exercise in speculation;" "The Martian Way" is "surely one of the best science fiction novellas ever published." He finds *End of Eternity* curiously uneven, with good ideas but some confusing exposition. Throughout, Knight gives good solid reasons—plot, characterization, background, etc.—for his opinions.

Lem, Stanislaw. "Robots in Science Fiction," in *SF: The Other Side of Realism*, Thomas D. Clareson, ed. Bowling Green, Ohio: Bowling Green University Press, 1971, pp. 307–333.

Lem's detailed study of the robot in science fiction contains the most negative comments found so far on the Three Laws. "I have forgiven Asimov many things," he says, "but not his laws of robotics, for they give a wholly false picture of the real possibilities." Lem maintains that a robot, to be intelligent enough to function effectively, would necessarily have to possess the intelligence to change his programme and could not be built with absolute safeguards against harming men. Not totally negative, Lem also cites "The Last Question" as one of the best science fiction stories with a religious theme.

Lundwall, Sam J. *Science Fiction: What It's All About*. New York: Ace Books, 1971. Translated from Swedish by the author.

A well-informed "outsider" looks at American science fiction. Asimov's work is mentioned much more frequently than the inadequate index indicates. Lundwall sees Asimov's Galactic Empire as a picture of the future that "makes all other imagined societies bleak in comparison" (p. 52), and recognizes the importance of his Three Laws.

Magazine of Fantasy and Science Fiction, XXXI (October 1966).

A special Asimov Anniversary edition. Asimov's article for this issue is autobiographical: "Portrait of the Writer as a Boy." He also contributed a new sf story, "The Key," and a poem about how young he was for such an old sf writer, "The Prime of Life." In addition, there is an Asimov bibliography and an appreciation by L. Sprague De Camp, both of which are listed separately here.

Miller, Marjorie. "The Machine in the Future: Man and Technology in the Science Fiction of Isaac Asimov." Unpublished MA thesis, University of Maryland, 1969.

Shows Asimov's basic faith in man's ability to overcome his problems; in spite of his interest in technological advances, Asimov believes that human nature and not technology holds the key to the future. Also describes the framework of galactic history into which most Asimov stories can be fitted.

Moskowitz, Sam. *Seekers of Tomorrow*. New York: World, 1966, pp. 249–265.

A biographical sketch, with particular attention to Asimov's career as an sf writer. Deals with John Campbell's role in the development of Asimov's talent, and with Asimov's niche in the sf pantheon.

Nathan, Paul, "Asimov's Hundred," *Publishers' Weekly*, CXCVI (August 25, 1969), 270.

A brief description of Asimov's career, occasioned by the publication of *Opus 100*. Ends with a comment on Asimov's failure to "capitalize on the lucrative market for pornography," and quotes Asimov's description of "Sally"—about a convertible that falls in love with a man—as "probably the sexiest story he ever wrote."

Nichols, Lewis, "Isaac Asimov, Man of 7,560,000 Words,"
New York *Times Book Review*, August 3, 1969, pp. 8, 28.

A description of Asimov's life and career. Superauthor in an attic—
90 wpm on the IBM electric, 8 hours a day, seven days a week; no
secretary, no agent, no vacations except under protest, does all
his own typing, reads his own galleys, answers his own mail. The
word count refers to *books* only.

"Overtaking the Future," *Newsweek*, LX (October 8, 1962),
104.

Science fiction viewed as prophecy, not as literature. Mentions *I,
Robot* as a "classic of the genre" and quotes Asimov as saying that
science fiction is "a topical fairy tale where all scientists' experiments
succeed."

Rogers, Alva. *A Requiem for Astounding*. Chicago: Advent,
1964.

A history of *Astounding Science Fiction* from 1930 until the name
change (to *Analog*) in 1960. Many references throughout to
Asimov. Rogers shows the possible connection between the robot
stories, set in the relatively near future, and the Galactic chronicles.
He sees *The Caves of Steel* and *The Naked Sun* as the bridge
connecting the two. A summary of the *Foundation* series is found
on pp. 177–180, but there is no critical analysis of the series.

Rose, Lois F. and Stephen C., "The Broken Circle: Science
Fiction and the Quest for Meaning," *Enquiry*, II (September–November 1969), 49–80.

Criticism with a particular aim—to find a religious message in
science fiction. The Roses discuss the *Foundation* series and *The
End of Eternity*, finding in them that Asimov assumes "that
humanity holds within itself over the long haul the key to its own
survival and happiness" (pp. 75–76). This long article was later
expanded into a book, *The Shattered Ring* (John Knox Press,
1970).

"Science Fiction: The New Mythology," [MLA Forum]
Extrapolation, x (May 1969), 69–115.

Chairman of the panel was Bruce Franklin; panelists were Darko
Suvin, Asimov, and Frederik Pohl. With Asimov as one of the
participants, there are references to his work throughout the
discussion. Asimov uses "Trends" to illustrate a point about sf as
prophecy, and the other speakers refer to it in reply. The prophecy
in "Trends" was strikingly right in predicting the first moon
flight for 1973, although Asimov thought it was highly optimistic,
and strikingly wrong in assuming that it would be accomplished
by one man building a rocket "out of tin cans" in his back yard
in secret.

"Scientific Inquiry: a *Boston* Interview with Isaac Asimov,"
Boston, LXI (December 1969), 51–54, 82–86, 89–90.

Asimov discusses prediction in his science fiction, mentioning the
moon trip in "Trends," and his views on the future of the world's
problems. He is fairly pessimistic about the possibility that
mankind might learn to solve its overpopulation, pollution, and
other problems before world-wide famine and other disasters
strike.

Tepper, Matthew B. *The Asimov Science Fiction Bibliography*.
Santa Monica, Calif.: The Chinese Ducked Press, 1970.

A complete listing of first appearances of Asimov's fiction to date
of publication, with alternate titles also given. No anthology listings.

Ulanov, Barry, "Science Fiction and Fantasy," in *The Two
Worlds of American Art*: *The Private and the Popular*.
New York: Macmillan, 1965, pp. 298–308.

Describes Asimov as "more trustworthy than most in his scientific
detail," and often completely absorbing. Says some of his stories
have "touches of Sholem Aleichem."

Williamson, Jack, "Science Fiction: Emerging from Its Exile
in Limbo," *Publishers' Weekly*, CIC (July 5, 1971), 16–20.

Science fiction as prophecy, not literature. Mentions Asimov as
one of the "semi-professional prophets of fact" that are being used
by business to project future worlds.

Wollheim, Donald. *The Universe Makers*. New York: Harper
& Row, 1971.

Describes Asimov's *Foundation* series as "the pivot of modern
science fiction," says that many writers since have used the
framework of the history of the Galactic Empire in their own stories.

Index of Asimov Titles

Axioms for Everybody, August
1957

BB or Not BB, That Is the
Question, August 1966
Backfire from speeding light, May
1967
Backward, Turn Backward—, May
1968
Balancing the Books, July 1966
Battle of the Eggheads, July 1959
Begin at the Beginning, January
1965
Behind the Teacher's Back,
August 1965
Belief, October 1953
Bessemer, January 1959
The Best New Thing, 1971
Bettering the Good Book, February
1970
Beyond Pluto, July 1960
Beyond the Phyla, July 1960
The Big and the Little, August
1944
The Big Bang, May 1958
The Big Number, February 1957
Bill and I, July 1971
The Billiard Ball, March 1967
Biochemistry and Human
Metabolism, 1952
Biological clocks, January 1969
The Birth and Death of the
Universe, see Over the Edge of
the Universe, March 1967

The birth of the oceans, July 1968
Black Friar of the Flame, Spring
1942
The Black of Night, November
1964
Blank! June 1957
Blind Alley, March 1945
Blood Will Tell, April 1962
The Bloodstream: River of Life,
see The Living River, 1960
Book reviews, Hornbook, August
1958 through December 1960
Bookworm, January 1971
Brazen Locked Room, June 1956
Breakthroughs in Science,
September 1958 through May
1959
Breakthroughs in Science, 1960
Breeds there a Man . . . ? June
1951
Bridging the Gaps, March 1970
Bridle and Saddle, June 1942
The Bug-Eyed Vonster, June 1960
Building Blocks of the Universe,
1957
—But How? November 1970
Button, Button, January 1953
Buy Jupiter, May 1958
By Jove! May 1962
The By-Product of Science Fiction,
August 1956

C-Chute, October 1951
C for Celeritas, November 1959

My Son, the Physicist, February 1962

The Mysterious Asteroids—"Vermin of the Skies," January 1964

Mystery of the one-way heat trap, May 1971

NASA Goofed! November 1969

The Naked Sun, October 1956

The Naked Sun, 1957

Names! Names! Names! December 1956

The Natural Occurrence of Short-Lived Radio-isotopes, December 1953

The Near East, 1968

Neglected Books, Spring 1970

The Neutrino, 1966

A neutrino is a neutrino, October 1969

Neutron stars—astronomical heavyweights, August 1970

The New Enzymology, May 1965

The New Intelligent Man's Guide to Science, see The Intelligent Man's Guide to Science, 1960

Nightfall, September 1941

Nightfall, and Other Stories, 1969

Nine Tomorrows, 1959

No Connection, June 1948

No More Ice Ages? January 1959

No Space for Women? March 1971

The Nobel Prize That Wasn't, April 1970

The Nobelmen of Science, April 1966

The Noble Gases, 1966

Nobody Here But . . . , 1953

Non-time Travel, June 1967

Not As We Know It, September 1961

Not by Bread Alone, May 1957

Not Final, October 1941

Nothing, March 1959

Nothing Counts, July 1964

Now Hear This! December 1960

Now You See It, January 1948

Nuclear Age Celebrates Silver Anniversary, December 1967

Obituary, August 1959

The Ocean Mine, March 1957

Of Capture and Escape, May 1959

Of Time and Space and Other Things, 1965

Oh, East Is East and West Is West—, March 1965

Oh, That Lost Sense of Wonder, January 1958

Old Man River, November 1966

On Flying Saucers, 1967

On Prediction, 1968

On Throwing a Ball, August 1969

One, Ten, Buckle My Shoe, December 1962

Only a Trillion, 1957

Opus 100, 1969

The Price of Life, January 1967
The Prime of Life, October 1966
Prime Quality, August 1971
A Problem of Numbers, May 1970
Profession, July 1957
The Proper Study, September 1968
The properties of cosmic rays and neutrinos and how they differ, February 1966
Protein, Key to Life, *see Chemicals of Life*, 1954
The Proton-Reckoner, January 1966
Pulsars—what are they? May 1970

Quick and Easy Math, *see Quick and Easy Math*, 1964
Quick and Easy Math, 1964

Races and People, 1955
Radioactivity of the Human Body, February 1955
Rain, Rain, Go Away, September 1959
Reaching for the Moon: An Introduction, 1971
Realm of Algebra, 1961
Realm of Measure, 1960
Realm of Numbers, 1959
Reason, April 1941
The Rebellious Stars, see The Stars, Like Dust, 1951
Recipe for a Planet, July 1961
Red Queen's Race, January 1949
Refraction vs. diffraction, July 1969

Rejection slips, 1959
Relative Contributions of Various Elements to the Earth's Radioactivity, January 1954
Relativity in 500 words, May 1966
The Rest of the Robots, 1964
Right Beneath Your Feet, January 1967
The Rigid Vacuum, April 1963
Ring Around the Sun, March 1940
Risk, May 1955
Robbie, *see* Strange Playfellow, September 1940
Robert Goddard, May 1959
Robot AL 76 Goes Astray, January 1942
The Rocks of Damocles, March 1966
Roentgen and Becquerel, February 1959
Roll Call, December 1963
The Roman Empire, 1967
The Roman Republic, 1966
The Romance of Mars, 1972
Round and Round and . . . , January 1964
Runaround, March 1942
Rutherford and Lawrence, May 1959

S, as in Zebatinsky, January 1958
SF as a Stepping Stone, August 1967
SF: Clue to Creativity, *see* The Sword of Achilles, November 1963

94

SF Market Still Healthy, August
1956
Sally, May–June 1953
Satellites in Outer Space, 1960
Satisfaction Guaranteed, April
1951
Science, F&SF, November 1958
through May 1972
Science Fiction, an Aid to Science,
Foresees the Future, May 1970
Science fictionally speaking,
January 1968
Science in Search of a Subject,
May 1965
Science, Numbers and I, 1968
A Science Seance, May 1969
The scientific method, June 1968
The Search for Other Planets,
April 1964
The Search for the Elements, 1962
The Sea-Urchin and We, July
1957
Second Foundation, 1953
The Second Revolution, 1967
The Secret Sense, March 1941
Seeing Double, December 1971
The Segregationist, 1967
The Sensuous Dirty Old Man,
1971
The Seventh Metal, January 1968
The Seventh Planet, March 1968
Shah Guido G, November 1951
The Shape of Things, September
1962
The Shaping of England, 1969
Shooting stars—fireworks in the
sky, August 1971

A Short History of Biology, 1964
A Short History of Chemistry,
1965
The Sight of Home, February 1960
Silly Asses, February 1958
The Sin of the Scientist, November
1969
The Singing Bell, January 1955
Sir Edward Jenner, January 1959
Sir Isaac Newton, November 1958
A sizable universe, November
1969
Slow Burn, October 1962
The Slowly Moving Finger,
February 1964
Social Science Fiction, 1953
The Solar System and Back, 1970
The Solar System and the Future,
see How Far Will We Go
in Space, 1966
Someday, August 1956
Sometimes You're Right, June
1957
The Sound of Panting, June 1955
Space Dictionary, 1971
Spacecraft, Like Squid, Maneuver
by "Squirts," July 1969
Speed Limit 186,300 MPS,
July 1969
Spell My Name With an "S,"
see S, as in Zebatinsky, January
1958
Squ-u-u-ush! November 1965
Starlight! October 1962
Stars, 1968
The Stars in Their Courses,
August 1970

DATE DUE

Printed
in USA

HIGHSMITH #45230